WONDER WHEELS

Through twelve hours of pouring rain

Wonder Wheels

THE AUTOBIOGRAPHY OF

EILEEN SHERIDAN

To the memory of my father,
a keen sportsman himself, who
always encouraged me to believe
that anything was possible

First published by
Nichołas Kaye Limited
194–200 Bishopsgate, London, E.C.2
1956

Re-printed in 2009 by
MERCIAN MANUALS LTD
353 Kenilworth Road
Balsall Common
Coventry, CV7 7DL.
www.mercianmanuals.co.uk

ISBN 978 1 903088 494

Contents

Illustrations

Acknowledgments

To *Cycling* for the frontispiece
To Len Thorpe for Plates 2, 3, 4, 5 and 21
To Ted Lees for Plate 6
To Fox Photos Ltd. for Plates 1 and 7
To The Scotsman Publications Ltd. for Plate 8
To the 'Topical' Press Agency Ltd. for Plate 9
To Hercules for Plates 13 to 21
To John Adams for Plates 18 and 20
To *John Bull* for Plate 22
To Keystone Press Agency for Plates 23 and 24
To the Central Press Photos Ltd. for Plate 25

Introduction *by* FRANK SOUTHALL

When Eileen Sheridan signed on for the Hercules Cycle and Motor Co. Ltd., I was asked to manage her road record attempts, and was told that the Company wanted a record as soon as possible.

Though I had naturally read and heard about Eileen's great amateur 12-hour rides, I had never seen her in action. When, therefore, on her first professional record attempt she went off course two or three times through sheer nervousness, insisted on being handed up cold drinks (though there was an icy mist during the early hours), and 'hammered' about all over the road when climbing Hindhead and Portsdown hills on an absurdly high gear, I thought to myself, 'What have I got here?'

But the last 20 miles of that first professional ride showed me in full measure the qualities which had enabled Eileen, as an amateur, to gain the title of British Best All-Rounder for two years in succession, and to ride $237\frac{5}{8}$ miles in 12 hours. I knew then that with the benefit of my experience of long distance road attempts, Eileen would go a long, long way.

And, indeed, the following three years proved this to be only too true, for she annexed all twenty-one records on the books of the Women's Road Records Association. Moreover, her rides were made in all weathers, for there was no waiting for the perfect day. The first suitable conditions were good enough for us.

The highlights of her great career were, of course, the Land's End to John O'Groats, and 1,000-mile records, followed after a few weeks' rest and speed training by the 50-mile and 25-mile records.

Throughout our association Eileen had complete trust in me to manage her attempts and to look after her, while for my part I had great confidence in her ability to tackle successfully any task that was required of her.

The helpers and I will never forget her supreme courage on the 1,000-mile record, and her determination to get there with a smile—there was never any question of 'packing up'.

From my point of view I have never seen anything so fine and great, and we glowed with pride to have been with Eileen on this ride of rides.

Quite apart from her record-breaking prowess, however, what must have been an extra reason for the Hercules Company to sign Eileen on was her charming personality and petite feminine appearance. Even on her 'End to End' ride, when any girl could be excused from appearing somewhat rough, her helpers remarked that through those three gruelling days she never lost her femininity.

Despite the fact that for three years Eileen has hit the headlines in the cycling world and has met some of the most famous people in the land, she still remains completely unspoilt, and is always ready to give advice and help to any young enthusiast who asks.

CHAPTER ONE

How it all started

The hotel porter was so surprised when he took charge of my bicycle and picked it up to carry it inside.

'Well I'm blowed,' he said, 'it weighs nowt at all.'

Then he looked at me and added, 'But I don't suppose you weigh much more yourself, do you lass?'

That was in 1953, and the bike he was talking about was the one on which I had just broken the London-to-York women's professional cycle record by riding the 196 miles in 9 hours 5 minutes and 20 seconds.

It was of course a good bicycle, a real lightweight, and quite different from the heavy old monster on which I had first started riding when I was a schoolgirl. In those distant days—well, it seems a long time ago now—a benevolent aunt passed on to me her discarded and rather ancient machine. Sedate and sluggish, it had the usual huge loop frame, big wheels, and handlebars that curved gracefully upwards and backwards—dignity expressed in ironmongery. As genteel as they made them.

On it I taught myself to ride, even though I wasn't big enough to reach the huge saddle (large enough to accommodate the most matronly of bottoms), and at every revolution of the pedals I rose and fell within the old-fashioned frame of the kind that nowadays is made only for export and sold in countries where bicycles are beasts of burden rather than the treasured instruments of recreation that we in Britain appreciate so deeply.

Yet, with all its faults and imperfections, it was that machine which first gave me a taste and an appetite for cycling. I was never allowed to take it out on to busy roads, but I learned to ride it. That was the beginning.

In those days—just before the second world war—I really was a little girl. But please don't misunderstand me. I was never puny. And nowadays, although it's true that I am only 4 feet 11 inches tall, and well-meaning people sometimes describe me as petite, I wouldn't call myself little at all. Not a giant, maybe, but definitely not little.

Still, I must admit that I was small when my father gave me my first real 'semi-sports' bicycle as a present on my fourteenth birthday.

What a bicycle it was too! Nowadays I don't suppose anybody would expect a child to push so much metal around, but at that time it was just what every loving parent would give to a daughter who longed for a bicycle.

What it weighed, I cannot say, but it must have been at least twice as heavy as the dainty little mount I handed over to the hotel porter at York, fifteen years later. Nevertheless, it was what I had asked for.

It was a bike, a real bike, and it opened up for me a brand new world of opportunity and delight. With it I explored the countryside around my Coventry home, and with it I learned to understand what a wonderful recreation cycling is—infinitely variable and absolutely inexhaustible in scope and pleasure.

Though I know now that my old bike must have been dreadfully hard to push, I did push it, and I thoroughly enjoyed pushing it, too. Admittedly, I remember that I used to stop for rests every ten miles or so, but what of that? I was in no hurry. I was discovering the world in which I lived and the fun of pedalling my way around it.

That bicycle made a real cyclist of me. It gave me the urge to wander down the lanes of Warwickshire, quietly yet more easily than I could have done on foot. It showed me what I myself could do to see and understand my homeland without the help (and the hindrance) of engines which give you more speed than you need and destroy the silence and intimacy of the cyclist's and the walker's contact with the countryside.

Speed didn't interest me very much in those early days. Now and again, it is true, I would bend down over the handlebars as I free-wheeled downhill, thoroughly enjoying the swift and silent swoop to the lower levels, but I seldom tried to get up any speed by pedalling.

The truth is that at that time I was not keen on hard riding, as I found out when a school friend told me that her brother would rather like to take me out on the back seat of his tandem. That seemed a good idea. He himself was a very keen cyclist, and going with him was grand fun.

Each time we went out our destination was a bit farther away, and I gradually began to realize that my pilot was deliberately increasing the mileages, because he was interested, first and foremost, in riding, and much less than I was in going places and seeing what there was to see on the way. There was no time to stop for a breather, and any halt 'to stand and stare' was a culpable waste of time.

For a girl who had done little cycling on her own that was a bit of a strain. In fact it was very much like hard work, because it never occurred to me to do less than my fair share of the pushing.

One day I remember very well. We set off early in the morning from my home in Coventry to ride to the Wrekin, in Shropshire, sixty miles away. And then ride back home again, of course.

As quickly as possible we covered the miles. Although it was a beautiful day, and there was so much to see on the way, we had no time for any frivolous dilly-dallying. We raced to the Wrekin. We rushed up that renowned beauty spot. We scrambled hurriedly through the Needle's Eye, a rock formation at the top, and after a few minutes pause, graciously conceded so that I might imbibe some of the splendour of the view from that glorious hill, we galloped down again to start the homeward ride.

For food, we had taken with us a few sandwiches which, after the morning's exertions, seemed most inadequate and left us longing for more. But they'd gone, and that was that, so off we set on the journey back to Coventry.

Ahead of us the sky began to darken. In a few minutes it looked ominous indeed. The horizon seemed to take fire, and trees, cottages, and farmhouses were silhouetted against the lightning that struck across the sky.

We could hear and feel the wind, growing fiercer every moment, yet not a drop of rain had fallen on us so far. But we knew it was coming and that we were in for a first-class storm.

Before it broke above us we entered a village, and there took shelter in a flagstoned passage by the side of an old cottage. Almost immediately the rain began to fall, though that is hardly the right word, for this time it seemed to be thrown down in uncontrolled and unlimited quantities. A swirling stream swept over our feet. The flashes of lightning became almost continuous and of terrible intensity, while the thunder sounded, and in fact felt, like a bombardment.

'Come in, come in; you can't stand out there.'

It was the owner of the cottage, a gentle little lady with a frightened expression, who spoke.

Gratefully we accepted her invitation, and for three hours we stayed in that little old cottage while the storm raged and thundered around us and the dear old lady sat white-faced and trembling in her chair.

Then, as the sky cleared and reality returned to the terrified world, we two cyclists set off again, thanking the old lady for her hospitality and leaving her to enjoy a cup of tea I had made at her request.

Late as we were, and uneasy at the time lost through that fantastic storm, I was rather glad that we had been able to pass the time with the little lady in the rocking chair. Alone, I'm sure she would have been terrified almost out of her wits.

We ourselves, now out on the open road again, were more than a bit uneasy. We were late. We had a long way to go. And we were hungry and penniless.

On through floods and mud-covered roads we pedalled, as fast as we could. We had to push hard, and I for my part did my utmost. In fact I began to realize that I was doing most of the pushing and looked like having to do still more before the day was out. My friend was beginning to sag.

Lack of food, and the physical misery it can cause, are known to cyclists by a number of funny names—the sags, the bonk, a packet, the knock, and so on—but the funny names cannot disguise the fact that the condition to which they refer is one of helpless, humiliating, incompetence. Legs seem to turn to string, and the most cheerful temperament is overwhelmed in pessimism and despair.

We came to a hill—steep and nasty. Obviously we had to walk. And while my companion staggered wearily along behind me, I pushed the tandem to the top.

It was then that I began to think I couldn't be such a bad cyclist after all, and to believe that my legs must have been made for the job.

It was late when I got home, and of course my parents were worried. Like many other parents in similar circumstances they showed their uneasiness in a burst of seemingly unreasonable scolding and 'this must never occur again, you understand'.

Quite right too, I say now. Especially as there hadn't been a drop of rain in Coventry all that gloriously sunny day.

But, you know, I enjoyed that outing.

CHAPTER TWO

Malvern Meanderings

Much as I was beginning to like cycling, it was still not my favourite sport. Swimming was what I liked most of all.

Almost every day, whatever the weather, I visited the local open-air pool, diving, swimming, and revelling in the water. On the whole, I really preferred the days when the weather was not so good, because there was then more room in the bath. It was the swimming that interested me, and not the other people who went there.

At any rate that was true until I began to notice that I was being noticed by a dark-eyed black-haired young man who swam and dived like an otter.

'You seem to come here quite a lot,' he said one day.

'Yes, I do. I love swimming.'

'What's your name?'

'Eileen Shaw. What's yours?'

'Ken Sheridan.'

He was a Londoner, working, like so many other engineers in those war years, in Coventry.

Regularly and as often as we both could manage it, we swam together in the local pool. Then, when the baths closed for the winter months, we went cycling together.

In 1942, after six months' engagement, we married. Eileen Shaw became Eileen Sheridan, and together the two of us became enthusiastic cycle tourists.

Happily, despite the solemn and uneasy times in which we were living, we toured the lanes of Warwickshire in our evening leisure hours and, at week-ends, went further afield.

A favourite week-end run was to the Malvern hills. There, in a cottage 800 feet up on the Herefordshire side of the range, we had a bedroom with an unforgettable view. Below us, where the hillside dropped away steeply, we could look down on the little villages that nestle so cosily in that charming countryside, and away in the distance there was the blue background provided by the Welsh mountains—a blue that often changed at sunset to an indescribable array of purples, orange, and flaming reds.

Everything and everybody was wonderful to us, in a land of loveliness and peace, set in the heart of a world at war.

The weather seemed always to be good to us, too, and I remember particularly one dazzlingly clear day when we left the cottage and climbed up to the highest point in the Malvern chain. The sky was blue and cloudless, and there in the distance we saw the unmistakable outline of Dunkery Beacon, on Exmoor.

In high spirits we returned to the cottage, and when our landlady remarked that we seemed to have enjoyed ourselves we told her of our good fortune at having actually seen Dunkery.

'Did you,' she commented. 'Well then, I reckon you won't be so lucky to-morrow. It'll rain all day.'

Both Ken and I agreed that that must be some 'old wives' tale' without any real foundation. We were enjoying a summer's day of the kind that is rare but usually repeats itself several times in succession when it does arrive.

Anyway, to-morrow would be soon enough to start worrying.

Some time during the night I was awakened by the sound of the wind whipping the curtains at our open window and by rain lashing my back. (As usual, Ken had got all the bedclothes tightly wound round him and I was out alone in no-man's land.)

'Ken,' I protested, and gave him quite a noticeable dig in the ribs; 'Ken, I'm cold, and it's raining on me. Could you close the window?'

He didn't hear. Or at any rate he didn't make any response. So I said it all again. I might as well have saved my breath. Ken was asleep, and when he's asleep, he's asleep.

I got up, wrestled with the window, and went back to bed. But before settling down I yanked all the clothes over to my side. It seemed to me that a man who could sleep as soundly as that didn't need clothes to keep him comfortable.

Next morning it was—of course—a grey and miserably wet day. Enshrouded in capes, we said goodbye to a lady whose weather-lore we both now respected very profoundly, and took the homeward trail through Worcestershire and Warwickshire.

On the way I began to feel sure that I should be able to do better if I could change my handlebars for a pair more akin to those used by the members of the cycling clubs we used to see so often. I knew, though, that my mother would have something to say against such an idea, though my father would probably just wink and keep quiet. As for Ken—well, I wasn't quite sure.

Faced with a problem like that most women would have done what I did. Without drawing anybody's attention to the change, I exchanged my handlebars for a pair that had a slight drop. It was a success right from the start, and as soon as my family had grown used to them I did another swap—this time increasing the drop just a little more.

It was a wonderful ruse, and in a few months time I fitted just the handlebars I wanted—beautifully curvaceous and almost bursting with potential speed and power.

Then Ken spoke. 'Now, look, Eileen,' he said. 'I've been watching you all along, and so far it's been jolly funny, but don't you really think these things are ridiculous?'

Squashed. Squashed as flat as a pancake. But not defeated. What I needed was the reinforcement of expert opinion to back me up. So we decided to join a cycling club.

As members of the Coventry and East Warwickshire district association of the Cyclists' Touring Club we met many other riders who shared our interest in cycling for pleasure, and of course most of them had far more experience than we had. With them we extended the scope of our week-end riding and began to understand that there was rather more in the cycling game than we had previously realized.

We discovered, too, that even the touring cyclists go in for competitions and trials of various kinds.

The C.T.C. has no direct interest in racing, and those members who want to take up that kind of sport must also join a specialist club (some of which are restricted to C.T.C. members), but it has produced a number of very distinguished racing cyclists.

A popular form of competition in the C.T.C. is what is known as a standard ride. It is not a race, and all the entrants ride together from start to finish, but they must cover a given distance in a stipulated time. A standard ride—a '140 in 12'—was being organized at the time when Ken and I first put on our winged-wheel badges and started riding with the local lads and lasses.

It seemed to us that an event of that kind would be good fun, so we filled up the entrance forms, paid over our entrance fees and looked forward to the great day when we should find out whether we really were capable of riding 140 miles in twelve hours.

CHAPTER THREE

The Fun of Club Life

When Ken and I rolled up for the start of the '140 in 12' our arrival seemed to cause some embarrassment.

Quite obviously the leader and timekeeper—the man whose job it was to 'nurse' the group and keep them all together—was uneasy. Some of the competitors also seemed doubtful in their minds, and one or two of them became almost fatherly towards me.

Nobody wanted to hurt my feelings, it appeared, but everybody wanted me to realize that I was the only girl entrant, and that 140 miles was quite a long distance, and that it had to be ridden in twelve hours, and that it would not be fair to the others if I kept the crowd back, and so on and so on.

I made it clear that I was going to ride, however, and that if I did drop behind at all they need not wait for me. Ken backed me up, and we all set off.

Actually I couldn't see what they were all so worried about. I knew I could do it.

After fifty miles or so the leader ceased inquiring at frequent intervals whether I was feeling all right and giving me little titbits of encouragement and advice—good advice, based on far greater experience than my own, but advice which I didn't heed particularly. We were out for a ride, and it seemed to me that the others were altogether too fussy.

At a hundred miles the leader accepted me as one of the gang, initiated and admitted to the inner circle, and let me know in confidence that he was now beginning to worry about some of the men wilting in the background.

Then, at the end of the ride, when I had qualified for my first cycling certificate and still wondered what all the solemn seriousness had been about, he gave me another bit of advice. 'If I were you, I should take up racing', he said. 'There's no telling what you could do if you tried.'

A good idea. I knew nothing about it, but it sounded like fun, so we looked around for a suitable racing club.

The following week-end Ken and I rode out to Edge Hill, in Warwickshire, to meet the Coventry Cycling Club at tea, to see what sort of riders they were, and find out as discreetly as possible whether I could keep up with them on the road.

The touring secretary gave us a warm welcome, introduced us all round, and told us something about the club and the kind of racing known as time trialling. Then, after a very satisfying meal, and in an air of complete understanding and friendship (the sort of friendship that you find in cycling clubs to an extent unknown in other sporting circles) we swarmed out of doors to get our machines for the ride home.

Ours, the newcomers' mounts, were naturally examined with profound interest. The angles, weights, and gearing were earnestly discussed, and Ken, who was very proud of his own steed, didn't emerge too badly from the examination.

My poor machine, however, seemed to cower under the inspection, and though nobody actually said anything that was really destructively critical, we knew quite well, my bike and I, that we'd been written off as not likely to be seen again.

The club had a tradition (as all good clubs have) of adjusting their pace to that of the slowest rider, and I learned afterwards that most of them groaned inwardly and wondered what time we should all get home. The only acceptable feature of my bicycle, it seemed, was the handlebars; they at least looked racy, but the rest of the machine, and above all the girl who rode it, seemed to have strayed into a world where they were sadly out of place.

Off we set, at a cracking pace. Riding in the usual neat and orderly two-by-two formation, we bowled along the smooth highway—a disciplined crowd under the leadership of a captain who knew his job. Tucked in at the back, Ken and I kept station proudly, thoroughly enjoying that indescribable sensation of almost noiseless motion and unity.

Right from the start the pace was fast, excitingly and satisfyingly fast, but gradually it seemed to increase. We were in fact 'winding it up', and later I learned the reason. Some of the lads had been surprised that the two novices hanging on behind had not yet dropped off, so they had quietly conspired to see how much we could stand.

Not knowing anything of that conspiracy, we turned the pedals round in an ecstasy of physical exertion, pulling strongly against the handlebars and wasting no breath in needless conversation. Hardly a word was said until the ride was over. Then I thanked them for a glorious experience. And I meant it, too. This was the life for me.

Every aspect of cycling club life turned out to be glorious. It was not all hard-riding, of course. There were quieter runs to places of interest, there were socials, dances, and clubroom evenings, and there were youth hostel week-ends.

On my first visit to a youth hostel our party included one other girl, Irene, whom I was very glad to see, especially as it meant I should have her company in the dormitory.

As we set off—a happy crowd of enthusiastic young folk looking forward to a week-end away from home—we didn't care what might happen. Rain or shine, we were going to have a good time together.

The pace was brisk, and soon I could tell that Irene, riding by my side at the back of the bunch, was having a hard time of it, trying to keep up with the boys. Gradually they drew away from us. I didn't like to leave her, and yet I didn't like to be dropped.

Then Irene herself solved the problem. Furiously she rang her bell—the recognized signal of distress—and sheepishly the speedsters dropped back and assumed a more sedate pace.

Lost in admiration of what I thought was her 'nerve', I said 'Ooh, Irene, I should never have dared to do that'.

'And why not, pray? This is a mixed club, and it's a club rule to make the pace suit the slowest riders, isn't it?'

She was right, of course, but that did not diminish my admiration for the girl who had made the lads wait for her, the girl who had brought them to heel, as it were.

The youth hostel we were heading for was at Broughton, in Northamptonshire. A fine old country house with lofty rooms and windows reaching from floor to ceiling, it impressed me immensely. There we unpacked our saddlebags, prepared our bunks, and then went down for a hearty meal in grand company—cyclists and walkers from a score of different places, all sharing the same love of the open air, and all good friends from the moment of meeting.

Towards the end of our meal the warden came to chat with us. He was not only the 'man in charge' of the old mansion frequented by young and very lively wanderers, but he also acted as gravedigger for the little priory church adjoining the hostel, and apparently the incongruity of the two sides of his life had developed in him a somewhat macabre sense of humour.

With spine-chilling dramatic effect he told us tales of the crypt—stacked high with human bones, he said—at Rothwell Church. They were blood-curdling stories, which he and we enjoyed together without taking them too seriously, despite his disconcerting trick of interrupting himself and solemnly hissing us into silence while he peered slowly round, as though afraid of being overheard by some ghostly intruder.

Those bedtime stories fresh in our minds, we retired to our bunks in the vast dormitory of that old, old house, with the churchyard hard by. And we slept like logs. For we were young and healthy and had ridden hard and eaten well.

In the morning, after breakfast, we reported to the warden to be told our duties—the little jobs that hostellers must carry out before going on their way. Some of us swept the floor or polished furniture. Others tackled the washing up, and all of us worked vigorously and cheerfully. Then came the farewells and cheerios, as cyclists and hikers departed for their different destinations.

Our little group rode off in search of the 'bone crypt' at Rothwell, about which the warden had told us so much the previous evening.

At the church we received permission to see the crypt, and were conducted through an ancient doorway and down a flight of stone steps. Then, in a cold and eerie atmosphere, we listened to more stories of that strange collection of human relics.

This time it was a warden of the church who recounted their history, or what was known of it. All around the walls of the large room were shelves loaded with skulls—nothing but human skulls. In the middle of the room was an enormous but neat pile of bones—arms and legs.

The bones had been found, we were told, buried only a foot below ground, at the side of the church. No one knew whether they were the remains of plague victims or of people slaughtered in a battle, but whatever the cause of their deaths they must have been veritable giants. The warden picked up one leg bone and placed it beside the tallest of the boys in our club, whose own leg seemed dwarfed by it.

He showed us also a number of bones that had been broken, and just before we left he took down from one of the shelves a big skull with a terrific dent in the top. Whatever weapon had caused that ghastly wound had penetrated deep into the brain of the wretched victim, and as we crowded round the 'exhibit' I for one felt that I had had enough of such contemplation. Perhaps my disquiet was visible in my face. At any rate I felt a hand, bigger than my own, gently closing around my wrist, and before I had time to understand the manoeuvre my outstretched fingers were thrust into the gaping fissure in that icy skull.

The laughter that followed was not at all convincing. Others besides myself welcomed the daylight and fresh air as we emerged above ground a few moments later. Once again, however, good hard riding and a hearty meal restored our natural exuberance, and as the day ended my only regret was that I should have to wait until the following week-end for another outing with that jolly crowd of good companions.

For Ken and me, club riding became one of the happiest features of a very happy life together. He, the Londoner, and I the Coventry girl, who had found so much pleasure in our comparatively leisured excursions awheel, were now tasting another delight in the infinitely variable cycling game. For us the bicycle was no longer merely a health-giving and inexpensive vehicle on which to explore the countryside, a link between city streets and quiet lanes; cycling was becoming a sport as well as a recreation and pastime.

Joyfully we used to tear through Stratford, Warwick, and Kenilworth with the racing boys. There was no time to admire the scenery. We thought only of the ignominy of being dropped and the satisfaction of proving ourselves as good as the rest of them.

Those hectic rides, those main-road 'bashes', were thrilling, satisfying, and at the same time inspiring. Yet the delight we found in them never dulled our love for gentle pottering in quiet surroundings.

Leafy Warwickshire may not be a county of spectacular scenery, but it can delight you with its gentle hills and noble parks, its historic castles and beautiful mansions. Ken especially loved its old villages and country towns, the thatched roofs and half-timbered houses. Whenever possible we would go riding together, but when that was out of the question one or the other of us would set off alone to visit once again some favourite spot within that county whose charms had first enticed us into the wonderful world of cycling.

On one of those solitary jaunts, when I had wandered quite a distance from home, I suddenly remembered an appointment in Coventry. Down went my hands on to the 'drops'. My fingers tightened round the grips, my forearms flexed as I pulled against the bars, and I put every ounce of my strength into the pressure on my pedals.

After the fastest ride of my life I reached home with just enough time to take a quick bath, change, and set off walking into town. As I strode out along the pavement, a man on a bicycle overtook me, glanced back, and then pulled up.

'Excuse me,' he said, 'But haven't you just been out riding on a bicycle?'

'Yes,' I replied, wondering what on earth was coming next. 'Yes, I've been out for a bit of a spin.'

'A bit of a spin! Three-quarters of an hour ago you passed me not far from Warwick, and as I didn't like the idea of being passed by a slip of a girl, I set off after you. But, by golly, you were too fast for me. And here I am, just arrived, while you've had time to change, and you look as if you'd never been on a bike in your life. It's—well, dash it, it's unbelievable.'

A few more words of conversation, and we went our separate ways. He was laughing and chuckling to himself. I was happy too.

CHAPTER FOUR

My Racing Career Commences

Ken bought me my first lightweight bicycle in August 1944. It was just what I wanted—a 'man's bike,' with light wheels and lively tyres. On such a machine I felt sure I could do something really worth while.

When the racing secretary of the club told me that a ten-mile time trial was to be held, and suggested that I ought to enter for it, I needed no persuasion at all. Already I had absorbed a good deal of the time-trial atmosphere, the sheer sportsmanship and camaraderie of all who follow the time-trial code.

It is, in my opinion, the finest of road sports. Competitors must go all out all the time. Every one of them rides alone, individually timed from start to finish. Released in number order, at intervals of one minute, their only aim is to cover the stipulated distance in as short a time as possible. No pacing is allowed. Spectators are not encouraged, and the races are held at times and places carefully chosen and kept strictly secret, so that no crowds may be attracted and so that the ordinary use of the roads by other traffic shall not be impeded.

In a smart red sweater and bottle green shorts, I presented myself at the start of the race. One of the boys suggested that it was time to change into my racing togs.

'What togs?' I asked. 'I'm riding in what I've got on.'

He was horrified.

'You can't do it,' he said. 'R.T.T.C. rules, you know. You've got to be inconspicuously clad, and your shorts and sweater must be black.'

That, I was told, was another of the strict rules imposed by the Road Time Trials Council to ensure that time trials were run for the benefit of the participants and not to amuse spectators.

So, after all, I shouldn't be allowed to ride. I was very disappointed, and rather more than somewhat critical of the man-made rules which I could not then understand. Why on earth couldn't I ride in my ordinary cycling clothes? Because it would make people look at me and realize I was racing, they said. A silly sort of argument it seemed to me, but of course I was not really in a mood to consider it dispassionately.

Then a young fellow rather shyly said he would be glad to lend me his alpaca jacket if I would like to borrow it. Bless his bonny face!

We were not built at all alike, and his jacket barely covered my chest, though it reached below my knees. Still, it solved my problem. After I had tucked up the hem and sleeves I was allowed to start.

Five-four-three-two-one- and away! I was off on my first time trial, riding as fast as I could for ten miles.

I won the race. As it happened I broke the club record too, so at the end of it all I was rather pleased with myself and my new bike and the club and—oh, everything, but especially was I pleased with the club, whose members were now our closest friends.

In their company Ken and I had some great larks during the following winter. Often I would be the only girl out with fourteen or fifteen boisterous lads—healthy and handsome young fellows who delighted in pulling my leg without mercy. But I had learned to take it. I was no longer the overawed novice afraid to open her mouth. I 'belonged'.

Naturally I was appointed chief 'pourer-outer of tea', and naturally, too, by the time I had distributed a cup to each of the boys there were some of them ready for a refill. Then, when I did at last get a chance to start my own meal, I discovered that my share of the cakes had disappeared. Oh, the lads were terribly sorry, of course. They wouldn't have done it if they'd known, and they thought I didn't like cakes, and I ought to think of my figure, and so on.

That was in the early days. In due course I learned to stake my claim before pouring out, and the boys had to sit and watch me catching them up when I had finished 'dishing out the tea'.

There was always merriment and laughter when we were out with the club. Even the little troubles and minor disasters that descend now and again on every cyclist can be treated light-heartedly in good company. What might dishearten a lone rider hurrying home late in the evening may prove quite amusing when there are others to share the misfortune.

One winter's evening we were all seated around a good fire at one of our favourite ports of call, at

Daventry. In a few minutes we should have to leave the cosy warmth of the cottage and face a brisk ride home. The first to break the circle got up and walked towards the window.

'I say, chaps, it's snowing. Come and look!'

It was, too. Large flakes were floating down in profusion on to ground already several inches thick with snow.

Whoops of joy and groans of dismay greeted this quite unexpected development. Members of another club who had had tea there shared our very mixed feelings, and when we set off on the homeward ride they joined us, the two groups forming quite an impressive procession of doggedly determined riders, picking their way over the white-carpeted road. It was tricky riding, but it was fun, despite the uneasiness in some of our minds.

After about seven miles of it the lads in front suggested a halt for something hot to drink. Our club thought it a good idea, but the others were more anxious to push on, so we wished them the best of luck as we ourselves gathered round a roadside cafe.

It was we who had the luck, for the driver of a lorry, realizing how difficult it was for us to push our way through the thick snow, offered us a lift. Gratefully, though with some pretence of self-criticism, we packed our machines in first and then clambered aboard the lorry. It had an open back, and as we sped rapidly on the way to Coventry we stood, tightly packed and somewhat unsure of our balance, looking backwards at the tracks made by the lorry in the glistening snow.

You should have heard the cheer we gave when we overtook the other club, still struggling manfully along. And you should have heard their counter-cheers, too!

During that same snowbound period we had a week-end at Astwell Castle youth hostel. Unique of its kind, it comprised one solitary remaining tower. Dining room and common room were on the ground floor, and to reach the dormitories there was a very narrow winding stone stairway, with a rope dangling from the top of the tower to serve as a handrail. If two persons met on the stairs, one of them had to back up or down to the nearest dormitory door to let the other pass.

There was no way of heating the upper rooms, and the wind whistled round the tower in a most chilling manner. To keep me warm that night I needed eight blankets on my bed. Yet I suppose our forebears were able to tolerate such bleak conditions.

Another memorable youth hostel week-end occurred early in March 1945. It was the occasion of the club's annual 'Van bash'—Van being the name of the hostel, 140 miles away in mid-Wales.

That ride was regarded as a very tough training spin for the boys who were looking forward to a season's road racing. It was definitely a run for the hardriders, a 'racing men only' outing, to be undertaken on the strict understanding that if any rider got left behind by the rest of the bunch he had to fend for himself.

As I too had made up my mind to enter for a few races that year, it seemed reasonable that I should join the lads on this occasion. We set off at a really hot pace, which never slackened the whole way, and by the time we had climbed the Clee Hills, in Shropshire, to the cafe where lunch had been ordered, we had appetites to do justice to a banquet.

After the meal we waited for a cup of tea, and eventually the good lady came in with one single cup.

'I can't manage tea for you all,' she said (it was of course rationed at that time). 'This is for the little lady.'

I thanked her and she withdrew. Immediately the boys began making offers for the tea, but though the bidding actually went up to half-a-crown, I explained regretfully that I really needed it myself.

Pressing on, we climbed Kerry Hill, on the borders of Wales, and then traversed the hilly road to Van youth hostel.

It was dark when we arrived there, to dismount with great relief and soon set about the hot meal prepared for us.

The hostel was without electricity, and I, the only girl there, had to find my way up to the dormitory by candlelight. There I chose a top bunk and made it comfortable with a pile of blankets. As the candle was practically finished, and seemed likely to stay alight only long enough for me to undress and climb into bed, I put it on the floor.

Dog-tired, I slipped between the sheets and waited for the candle to go out. But it had no intention of leaving me in the dark. For at least a quarter of an hour its flickering light illuminated the dormitory, where I, alone among all the unoccupied bunks, was longing only for darkness and sleep.

At last I could stand it no longer. I should have to

put the confounded candle out. But how could I do it without leaving my warm bunk and braving the icy draughts which the cold March wind was creating in the room?

Leaning over the edge, I waved one of my long cycling socks vigorously over the flame, hoping to dowse it in that way, but the candle was not so easily discouraged. It was used to draughty conditions, and continued to shed its fluttering light around. Then, in desperation, I threw the sock straight at it.

That did the trick. Darkness surrounded me at last, and with a sigh of relief I snuggled deeper into my bedding. At that very moment the door opened quietly, and in came a girl carrying a nice bright candle.

I could have screamed. But she was so polite and friendly. 'I'm sorry to disturb you,' she said. 'I tried to come in quietly because the warden told me there was a schoolgirl asleep up here.'

Next morning, after rising early and carrying out our hostel duties, we set off on the return journey. A Leamington club, also out on a training spin, joined us after a while, and one of the lads who was having rather a hard time appealed to me for a little assistance.

'Here, lass, give us a bit o' your back wheel.'

For the rest of the way he rode right behind me, thus keeping out of the wind, and when the two clubs parted company he shouted to all of our chaps: 'That lass ought to take up racing. She can go.'

They agreed. By that time everybody seemed to

think it was inevitable that I should take up time-trialling.

My first open 25-mile race (that is to say, open to other clubs as well as my own) was tremendously exciting. I was to be the first off, and, as a novice, I had a handicap allowance of nine minutes. A men's race was being held before our event, over the same course.

The start of the women's race was fixed for 8 a.m. at a place about fifteen miles from my home, so Ken and I rose early that morning in order to get there in good time. If Ken hadn't been going with me, I don't think I should have got there at all, so weak was I with nervousness. He had to help me all the way.

A crowd of club cyclists had assembled at the start to watch and cheer the riders off. As I mounted my machine I trembled so much with nervous tension that I could hardly get my feet into the toe-clips, and the official who was holding my bicycle tried to encourage me by saying, 'I think you're going to do well; you see if I'm not right.'

The timekeeper's voice broke in. 'Ten seconds to go.' Then 'five, four, three, two, one—go,' and I was off, pedalling like mad and gasping for breath.

In a very short time I began to settle down and feel at ease. My nervousness vanished and I thought only of riding, riding as fast as I could.

The course was centred on Stonebridge, between Birmingham and Coventry. It had three distinct 'legs': out and back to Stonebridge, out in another direction and back, and finally out to the last turn and back to the start again.

At the final turn the official who was checking the riders' numbers expressed astonishment that I, an absolute beginner in the racing game, should still be well in the lead, with only four and a half miles to go. I was in fact only a few minutes' riding from the finish of the race when I encountered the first of the other girls making her way to the last turn. Then, of course, I realized that I must be doing pretty well, and, to confirm the belief, I actually overtook one of the riders in the men's event before I came to my own finishing point.

I had tried. I had tried as hard as I could, and I felt that I hadn't disgraced my clubmates. But can you imagine my excitement when it was announced that I had not only won the handicap prize but also the award for the fastest actual time!

Ken and the other members of my club were literally jumping with joy at my success in my very first open event.

CHAPTER FIVE

Success in My First Year

After two more wins in the Midlands I decided to enter for an important ten-mile race south of London.

When I received my start sheet I was delighted to see that I had been put on the scratch mark. That meant that all the other riders' handicap allowances were based on my fastest time, and it was of course an indication that I had made my mark in women's time-trial circles.

The London girls gave me a warm welcome on my first incursion into their territory. Many of them were inclined to think, though, that with a full start card of a hundred riders, and in view of my lack of experience, my position as scratch girl was an error of judgement on the part of the handicapper.

The night before the race Ken had given my legs a thorough massage. I felt terribly keyed up, but was in good form, and once again I rode and won.

Ken claimed that the massage had had a lot to do with it. Perhaps it had. I don't know, but I often remind him that during the last two years of my amateur racing career he didn't massage me at all, and yet I became faster.

Success doesn't come easily, though, and I did in fact train very hard for my races.

I travelled all over the country, and had keen

tussles with the reigning champion, Susie Rimmington. The week before the women's national 25-mile championship I managed to beat her, but by only a narrow margin, on the actual course to be used for the championship.

On the morning of the championship race itself, the atmosphere was tense indeed. During most events, when travelling in opposite directions, Susie and I used to grin and nod at one another, but this morning was different. I was riding harder than ever before. As we met we both automatically glanced at our watches, and there was no doubt at all that we both meant very serious business.

Well, it happened to be my day, and I became champion in my first year of racing.

I shall always admire Susie Rimmington. Her consistently fast rides made me try every inch of the way whenever we rode together, and so improved my performances enormously.

In one 50-mile race Susie was listed to start only three minutes behind me (an unusual arrangement, because 'fast markers' are normally spaced out at ten-minute intervals). It was obvious that she would do her best to catch me, or at least to get a good lead and stick to it. Still, I decided to ride my own race and not to worry unduly, even though I am usually a slow starter.

There were three dead turns on that course, and I could see that at the first and second Susie had gained about a minute and a half. At the third turn, however, I had only just rounded the marshal when I saw her there, right on my tail!

'Susie,' I gasped, and covered the last ten miles as

though it had been the devil himself that was chasing me.

Word had gone round that there would be a fighting finish. It didn't work out that way, though. Susie came in two and a half minutes after me, to gasp, as she rested on her machine, 'I'm all in!'

All in or not, she had held the lead gained by her terrific effort earlier on, and I took second place.

It was in events like that that I learned how to race, enjoying every minute of it.

I recall one very wet morning when I was due to start in a Midland 'fifty' and saw some of the club boys rubbing their legs with a concoction they were pouring from a large bottle. Personally I usually rubbed olive oil into my limbs, to try to keep the damp coldness from affecting the muscles, but on this particular morning I had forgotten it.

'Would you like some of this?' asked one of the boys.

'Is it any good?'

'Any good! This is super-special stuff. It's what they use on horses. This'll really make you go.'

That sounded encouraging, so I joined the rubbing party.

The first girl in my event was to be sent off ten minutes after the last rider in the men's race, and I was to start last of all the women. Everybody was thus in front of me when I set off.

Though the morning was wet and miserable, my legs felt warm enough and were working well. After catching and passing all the girls, I could see in the distance one of the riders in the men's race. Gradually I overhauled him too. Then, just as I was about to pass him, I felt suddenly embarrassed and shy. Whatever would he think? What on earth could I say to the poor man? He must be taking a dreadful hiding.

As I drew alongside he looked sadly at me, but made no remark.

'Golly, isn't it tough?,' I said.

His reply was a short and hollow laugh.

By now the horse liniment with which I had anointed my legs was burning and irritating them most painfully, so I fairly flashed along. The sooner I finished the course, the sooner I should be able to end the torture.

Before I reached the crowd clustered around the timekeeper in the pouring rain I had overtaken two more men, but without waiting to find out what my time had been for the fifty miles, I dashed off to the changing rooms. There I washed off the embrocation that had caused so much discomfort, whatever its effect on my speed might have been.

If it really was something they use on horses, I can only say that whips and spurs must be kinder.

Training for those week-end racing activities had to be done during the evenings, for I had a full-time job as secretary to the sales manager of a large motor-car showroom in Coventry. Each morning, before I left home to cycle to the office, I did the housework and regularly baked a cake or two, so that the evenings would be free for my cycle training.

The policeman on point duty at Broadgate, Coventry's main thoroughfare, was so accustomed to seeing me in a tearing hurry in a morning that he would wink at me and say 'Late again!' as I went flying past.

Adjoining the showroom was a service garage, approached by a wide drive, off which a glass door led straight into the showroom itself. That was my way in, and as the door was usually open, instead of dismounting from my cycle in the entrance drive, I used to cycle in and across the showroom floor. Only the office door—always closed—stood between me and a spectacular dismount right at my desk.

One morning when I had had an extra large amount of work to do at home, and was therefore particularly late for the office, I saw as I approached the garage drive that three people were standing between me and the showroom door with their backs towards me. Hardly slackening my pace, I wove my way in and out of the available space, disappeared into the showroom, and settled down at my desk, very businesslike and confident that no one who mattered had noticed my late arrival.

A few moments later the general manager came in. He not only pointed out that I was late, but also informed me that it gave a bad impression when employees indulged in trick cycling round the managing director, the sales manager, and the general manager.

Quite a delicate situation—but fortunately the general manager was blessed with a sense of humour. Moreover, realizing that it was no easy task for me to run a home and do a full-time office job, he very generously allowed me time off every week after that, to help me out.

I think everybody was kind to me in those days.

Certainly, looking back on that period of my life, I realize not only how happy I was, but also how much my happiness was due to the fact that I was surrounded by friendly people who seemed only to want to assist and encourage me—at home, at work, and in the club.

In November I was invited by the Road Time Trials Council to the champions' concert at the Royal Albert Hall, to receive the magnificent national 25-mile trophy. That was an occasion I had envisaged only in my wildest dreams, and never shall I forget it. To the cheers of thousands of cyclists—enthusiasts for the greatest of all outdoor games—I stepped on to the stage, received my award, and was then asked to say a few words.

What could I say? What could anybody say on an occasion like that, except 'thank you'—thank you to the grand lads and lasses who so warmly applauded my success, but thank you even more to those who had made my success possible, those who had helped and encouraged me, those who had taken me to their hearts and steeped me deeply in the loyalties, the traditions, and the friendships of the cycling world.

Leaving the hall after the concert I saw Miss Marguerite Wilson, then holder of nearly all the women's professional road records. Nervously, I asked for her autograph. It never occurred to me that some day I might myself be making attempts on those same records. Already I was looking forward to the birth, in the new year, of my baby.

As 1945 drew to its close, I could not stifle a feeling of regret that such a happy and longed-for event would also put an end to my racing career.

CHAPTER SIX

My Son Clive

Many sporting people, I imagine, keep a scrapbook. I do, anyway, and if you turn back the pages to April 1946 you will find there a large safety pin surrounded by cuttings headed 'SPECIAL NEWS'. For it was on 5th April of that year that my son Clive was born—by Caesarean operation.

Lest it be imagined that the operation was necessary because of my extensive cycling activities, I hasten to point out that it was actually due to the heftiness of the infant and the smallness of my pelvic cavity. In the weeks preceding Clive's arrival I was very fit indeed. In fact, the day before he was born I enjoyed a spot of digging in the garden in the lovely spring sunshine.

At the hospital, when I was eventually allowed to get up and carry my baby to and from the nursery, the nurses declared that he was nearly as big as me!

And what an occasion it was when I went home with the new addition to our little family! The happiness, the excitement, and the pride as friends called to see my little boy. Then someone said 'You'll have finished with cycling now, Eileen, I suppose'.

Yes, I had to admit, the doctor had given me strict orders not to cycle for at least a year.

I regained my strength in a surprisingly short time,

however, and one warm spring day—just seven weeks after Clive's birth—the longing to go riding again became irresistible. I was sure it would do me no harm. In fact I believed that a gentle ride would do me a lot of good.

Ken was doubtful. So were my parents. But, on the firm condition that it would be only a little ride and that I should not overtire myself, it was agreed that Ken and I should go and meet the club, just to ride a little way with them, while my parents looked after the baby.

How pleased everyone was to see us after my enforced absence! And how pleased we were to be with them again, as we rode off, immersed in the usual light-hearted conversation of a club run.

Ten miles went by. Then twenty.

Ken said I ought to turn back now, but I felt fine and pleaded to be allowed to continue. Although I couldn't keep up with the club on the hills, I could catch them again on the level stretches. He yielded, and we spent the whole day with them. Every minute of that eighty-mile run in the Cotswolds was a delight.

It was not very long before Clive was riding with the club too. When he was five months old we started taking him out for gentle rides in the country—snug and perfectly safe in a natty little trailer behind Ken's bike. There, gently rocked by the motion of the wheels, and lulled by the changing scenery, he would gurgle with delight and drum with his little feet on the sides of the trailer for a short while, before dropping off into peaceful slumber.

As he grew older we had to make sure that he was

well strapped in, for he would try to stand up or hang over the back as we went bowling along. His toys, too, had to be tied on, to prevent him from strewing them all over Warwickshire.

We sold the trailer when he became too heavy for it and acquired a basket-seat that could be attached to Ken's bike or to mine. With Clive thus seated behind me, I was climbing a hill in Coventry one day, swinging my weight from pedal to pedal—not very stylish, I admit, but I did not want to get off and push—and of course he too was swaying slightly from side to side. Then suddenly he piped up merrily from behind me: 'Heave ho, my hearty!' So I had to get off—to laugh.

Eventually, of course, Clive grew too big and heavy to be taken as a passenger on a bicycle. Then, when I went racing, my father and mother would look after him. More often than not they would take him out in their car to watch me.

Gradually my old fitness returned and I began to regain my former speed. Riding became more and more enjoyable, and often, when I had put Clive to bed, Ken would put my racing bike outside the gate and suggest that I should go for some fresh air and exercise on my own. One day when I was out on one of those trips a boy from a rival club saw me. 'Ah', he called out, 'secret training, eh? I shall tell 'em.'

Though I laughed, it was not far from the truth, and in September—less than six months after Clive's birth—I again entered for a ten-mile race. Clive was there at the finish to see me win—and how the racing girls were spoiling him, too!

Winter came, and we began to think of the 1947

racing season. If I did decide to do a spot of racing, said my father, he would always be glad to look after 'Junior'. If I did! He knew very well he was aiding and abetting me to do just what I wanted to do.

Ken, a keen gymnast, and very interested in weight-training, persuaded me to try my hand at exercising with lightly-loaded barbells and dumb-bells. As a result, my strength increased considerably, and occasionally, just for fun, I used to go all out. I was able to heave a barbell loaded to almost my own body weight (eight stone) from the floor to arms' length overhead, and could press a 60-lb. barbell ten times in succession.

As a spectator, I paid one or two visits to the Butts cycle track in Coventry. There my interest in track racing was aroused and I began to enter for the Midland Sports League evening meetings, where I had as rivals most of the female track exponents from the Coventry and Birmingham area.

By now Clive was a toddler, and while I was tearing round the track in the various races, he loved to play about on the grass centre, under my father's watchful eye. His favourite game was jumping into the long-jump pit. He would take such a terrifically long run that by the time he reached the pit he was quite exhausted, and could only collapse in a happy heap on the soft sand, greatly to the amusement of the spectators in the stands.

Unintentionally, I too amused the spectators on one occasion. It was a particularly chilly evening, and I was sitting on the green in my track-suit awaiting my heat. My number was called, and I hurriedly removed my suit, not realizing that in doing so I had pulled my long white track vest right down over my shorts. To the onlookers I appeared to be wearing nothing but the vest.

The jocular remarks fired at me from all directions were the first indication that I had done anything unusual.

On the track in the Midlands my chief rival was Muriel Maitland, wife of Bob Maitland, one of the foremost British riders. Muriel had the track exponent's ability to 'jump' her bike, making it leap forward when neck-and-neck with an opponent very close to the finishing line. On several occasions she jumped to beat me by a few inches, but I hadn't mastered that technique. My method was to increase my pace steadily right from the start, in the hope of wearing out my opponent. From the spectators' point of view it was hardly thrilling, but it enabled me to win a considerable number of events.

In 1947 the Midlands 1,000-yards women's sprint championship was held at the Butts track. To win it, Ken said, I should have to use all my wits as well as my strength and so, long before the event, I began to plan my campaign. One day, giving the matter very serious thought as I washed up, I figured it all out. In my mind's eye I could see the track, the riders, and the race. As we all went whizzing round I knew just what to do. 'This is where I make my all-out effort. Now!'

I came out of my daydream with my heart beating as if I really had just finished the race, and realized that, as the tempo of my imaginary race had quickened, I had been piling crockery on to the draining board at an alarming rate.

On the day of the championship I was one of eight girls lined up for the 2½-lap race. The starter fired his gun, and we were off, but no one seemed keen to take the lead. In my determination not to be boxed in, I took up a position on the outside of the bunch and remained there until, with nearly a lap to go, I shot forward in an all-out effort to open up a gap sufficiently great to make it difficult for an opponent to catch me before the finishing line.

The trick worked. None of the other girls imagined I would make a break with more than three hundred yards to go, and so I crossed the line more than two lengths ahead of Muriel. Just as I had done at the kitchen sink!

Although I won a number of road events in 1947, absolute peak fitness evaded me, and in the national 25-mile championship I could manage only fourth place.

Still, I was not dispirited. It was rather too soon after Clive's birth to expect a full return of my former speed. In any case, I had many more seasons of racing to look forward to.

CHAPTER SEVEN

Two Full Seasons

In 1948 the Road Time Trials Council inaugurated a women's best-all-rounder competition, on similar lines to the existing men's B.A.R. The winner would be the girl who set up the fastest average speed in races at 25, 50, and 100 miles, and I was determined to have a darned good try at being the first to get the title of British Best All-Rounder.

In a fifty-mile event on the Bath Road, one miserably wet morning, I misjudged the greasiness of the road at the far turn and crashed heavily. The marshal helped me up, asked if I was all right, received a reassuring reply, and assisted me on to my machine again. There were twenty-five more miles to go, but it was not until I had covered about half that distance that my forearm began to ache painfully. My injury was greater than I had realized, and after crossing the finishing line I rolled up my sleeve to find a really nasty gash on my arm.

It is difficult to estimate how much time I had lost, but I had to be content with second place to Stella Farrell—another great opponent of mine—by a matter of two minutes.

After numerous successes at 10, 25 and 50 miles, I persuaded Ken to let me ride in a 100-mile race—again on the Bath Road. On the night before, I stayed at an old thatched cottage near Pangbourne, a Thames-side village, sharing a bedroom with three other girls—two from Oxford and one from London.

My main anxiety before competing in that, my first long-distance event was that I should suffer from hunger during the five hours or so of riding. Hunger 'knock', the sudden weakness which overcomes a rider whose system is demanding more fuel in the form of food, can be so overpowering that a rider may find it impossible to continue.

'Oh, yes, you must eat as much as you can before going to bed,' said my room-mates. They had had previous experience of long-distance races, so I took them at their word.

Until the early hours of the morning I sat up, stuffing myself with biscuits, sultanas, chocolate, and vegetarian dried fruit blocks (though I'm not a vegetarian). It really was a gargantuan guzzle.

Then I slept.

When I awoke the branches of a tree in the garden were being beaten against the bedroom window, in which four glum girls were far from happy at the prospect of battling with the elements for a hundred miles.

As usual before an event, I just toyed with my breakfast, while my friends insisted that I must eat everything that the helpers handed up to me during the race. With that advice ringing in my ears, I set off to the start.

At certain points along a long-distance course there are 'feeding stations', where groups of keen club-folk hand food and drink to the riders. The helper sprints alongside the rider to enable him to snatch the packet or flask as the case may be, without slackening speed more than absolutely necessary.

The first packet handed to me contained cheese-and-tomato sandwiches. Next came a large bag, into which I delved and discovered two tomatoes and three pears. I hastily stuffed this bag into the breast pocket of my sweater, but as I leaned over my handlebars the heavy fruit dangled and banged about on the top tube of my machine. The only thing I could do was to eat it as fast as I could, with the result that my tummy felt so uncomfortably full I had to sit up for a short time.

When, to my horror, yet another large brown bag was offered up to me—peaches and a slice of melon, they said it was—I had to refuse it politely but firmly, for I had begun to realize I was losing time by eating so much. Hunger knock or no, I had to ride fast and forget the food.

As I went over the finishing line and called out my number, I felt that my first hundred had really been an enjoyable experience. Then, when the last girl had finished, it was announced that I had won the race by over two minutes from my formidable opponent Susie Rimmington, with the third girl a further nine minutes away. Incidentally, I had just missed the national competition record figure by a minute.

My friends of the previous night were thrilled with my performance. They believed that their leg-pulling, which had led me into my all-night eating session, had done the trick. Perhaps they were right. At any rate I had escaped the hunger knock!

After that experience I was most eager to ride another 'hundred', but there are not many events at that distance, so I had to wait until the following year.

There were several keen racing girls in the Coventry Cycling Club, and they supported me enthusiastically in a number of events ranging from ten to fifty miles. We had numerous triumphs as a team and rounded off the 1948 season by breaking the national team competition record at thirty miles. I myself gained the individual national record at that distance with a time of 1 hour 19 minutes 28 seconds (which still stands at the time of writing).

The close of that very energetic season saw us in possession of six team awards, while I had fourteen first and six second placings. But in the national 50-mile championship I had managed only second place. In the best-all-rounder contest, too, I had to concede a victory to Susie Rimmington. Her average speed over the three distances worked out at just ·008 m.p.h. faster than mine. What a tussle, and what fun!

On the track I had won an award every time I made an appearance. My ambition, however, was to attempt a 12-hour ride on the road. The women's record stood at 220½ miles, and after my 'hundred' I felt sure that I could last out half a day and get somewhere near that figure. Ken was of a different opinion, though, and despite my pleadings, insisted that I should wait until the following year, by which time I should have gained more experience.

The year 1949 proved exciting and successful for me, but my triumphs were achieved only after vigorous sessions of weight training and gym in the cold winter months, followed by intensive training spells on the road as soon as the weather became warmer.

Although I have never considered myself a first-class 25-miler, I usually managed to be placed, and in the 1949 national 25-mile championship I gained third place and helped the Coventry C.C, girls to team honours. Later in the year our team also broke the 25-mile competition record.

July and August seem to be the months in which I do my best rides, and it was during that period that I annexed the national 50-mile competition record with a time of 2 hours 16 minutes 1 second. A little later I was runner-up in the 50-mile championship.

To get into the best-all-rounder contest I had to compete in a 'hundred', and there was only one event at that distance in which I could ride during the year. So once again to the Bath Road, for the Twickenham 'hundred', and, remembering the previous attempt, I decided to prepare myself again by over-eating. Then, before setting out for the start, I put two dried-fruit bars in my breast pocket, to make sure that I should last the course without wasting so much time sorting out the large bags handed up during the event.

Of course I had been hoping for a really warm August morning, so that I could put up a decent time to help in the B.A.R contest, but it turned out very wet and windy. It was so wet that I could not stick my schedule (which Ken always works out for me to ride to) in its usual place on the top tube of my machine. It just refused to stick at all, and as the timekeeper called out 'half-a-minute to go, Eileen', I thrust the schedule into my pocket with the fruit bars, intending to look at it from time to time during the race. Actually, though, I forgot all about it.

The rain was very heavy indeed. Mud was splashed all over my face, because the mudguards had been removed from my machine to reduce wind resistance. And my fruit bars, which I munched during the race, had become very gritty and horribly wet and sticky. The rice paper on them seemed particularly tough, and, having difficulty in chewing them, I gulped the lot down and left my tummy to sort things out.

At the finish, completely soaked to the skin, I found that I had eaten not only my fruit bars but also the schedule. No wonder they had been tough to chew! It was all for the best, though, because the schedule had been worked out for a calm morning, and it would have been disheartening to attempt to ride to such fast figures when battling against severe winds and torrential rain.

My time was four minutes slower than the previous year's performance, but I had again accomplished the fastest 100-mile ride of the year, and beaten my challenger by nearly six minutes.

Six days after that 'hundred' I entered for the Women's National Sprint Championship, held at the Butts track, Coventry. I got through my heat and semi-final, and in the final was opposed by two London girls—Ann Hunnisett, holder of the title, and Daisy Stockwell. A typical road girl, I allowed myself to be boxed in, and only by dropping right back and putting up a fight on the finishing straight did I manage to gain second place to Miss Stockwell.

My interest now turned to a 12-hour event, and my club were very anxious to see me ride, because I had shown no signs of exhaustion after the 'hundred'. Indeed, after the last effort I actually rode forty miles back to the home of Ken's people in Richmond.

The event that I longed to enter was held right up in the north, and it is of course expensive to travel to ride on fast courses all over the country. Besides, Ken pointed out, a 12-hour race was not necessary for the B.A.R., and in any case we were buying a little house in Coventry—and in addition to the cost of travelling there was also the accommodation for the night to pay for.

Though I had to agree, I was disappointed, and during the week, when I went along to the clubroom and some of the keen long-distance men asked if I had entered for the Yorkshire 12-hour, I must have looked very sorry for myself. After I had explained that it was rather awkward for me, Laurie George, the Club's racing secretary, said 'Stay there, Eileen. Don't go away till I come back.'

When he returned, his face shining, he had a form in his hand.

'Listen, kid,' he almost shouted. 'You fill in this entry form. Seven of us will go up to Wetherby to help you in the race, and the expenses for you and Ken will be covered.'

Bless him! I could have cried with joy, but I still had to talk Ken into the idea that a 'twelve' wouldn't hurt me. That wasn't difficult, and I shall never be able to thank those club boys enough for giving me the chance to ride in the race which was perhaps the one that started me on my long-distance record-breaking career.

CHAPTER EIGHT

A 'Twelve' at Last!

Twelve hours in the saddle! That would be no picnic, whatever the weather. Previously I had ridden for only just under five hours while actually racing, so, the weekend before my long-for attempt at a twelve-hour ride, Ken sent me out on a marathon training spin.

Feeling extremely fit, I set off. About fifty miles from home I began to overtake some male riders taking part in a time trial. After I had passed several of them, I learned that the event in which they were riding was an inter-club 12-hour race. Some of the riders looked very fatigued. How should I feel the following weekend? I returned home and for the rest of the week took things easily—at least, I did no cycling.

The running of a 12-hour event calls for numerous cycling club people to marshal the course, so that competitors cannot go wrong on any difficult parts. Should anyone actually go off course, the extra mileage he covers cannot be claimed. Checkers are scattered about on the roads at different points, and to them the cyclists call their numbers. Their times are recorded as proof that they have completed the full course.

After about 200 miles the riders are sent round a

finishing circuit where timekeepers are usually positioned roughly every three miles. As each competitor nears the end of his twelve hours of riding, one of the timekeepers sends a cyclist, with a watch set to his own, to ride behind the finisher and stop him when the twelve hours have been completed. The finishing spot is noted, and then the mileage officially worked out.

Ken went with me by train to York, and from there we cycled the fourteen miles to Wetherby. It was pouring with rain when we reached our 'digs'. But someone was happy: one of a number of racing men, also staying there, came over and grinned at me as he watched Ken strip my cycle ready for the morning.

'The women have the worst circuit' he chanted gleefully. 'The women have the worst circuit.'

It turned out that there was a men's event over the same course. But because of a rule which forbids men and women to race on the same roads at the same time, we were to be sent on enormous circuits in different directions, ending with separate finishing circuits of about twelve miles in length.

The morning was beautiful—despite a cold early mist—and I was ready for any circuit. Nothing mattered now except that at last I had the chance to tackle what I had always longed to do.

There to cheer me and help me were the Coventry boys—my clubmates who had made it all possible. Five of them had travelled to York in the early hours of the morning in the racing secretary's van; a sixth had ridden through the night.

'Just ride, kid, and don't worry,' they called to

me, and I felt a lump come into my throat. Ride I must; I couldn't let them down.

Yet I very nearly did. Probably due to nervousness or overkeenness, I did a very silly thing. Somewhere in the first twenty-five miles I had a horrible feeling that I had gone off course. I hadn't seen anyone for a time, and in a panic I turned round and began to cycle back furiously. In about three-quarters of a mile I came to a fork road, but there were no signposts and no one was about. A motor-cyclist came along, so I waved him down and asked the way to York. His answer showed that I had been right all along. All I had done was to waste precious time.

Ashamed of myself, I rode strongly, but when I passed the boys at the 25-mile point I could see they were worried. Whoever was leading, it certainly wasn't me. At length, however, I began to overtake girls who had been sent off at two-minute intervals before me.

At sixty miles my rival Susie Denham, who had started ten minutes ahead, was in sight. This rather shook me, and my husband thought I must be overdoing things—for Susie was the national 12-hour record holder with a distance of 220½ miles.

'Don't pass her,' he called out, as, at a road junction ahead, he got out of the van being driven by Laurie George, our racing secretary. 'You'll never last the course.' He held out a banana. 'Stop and eat this,' he pleaded.

I refused to stop, but decided that, if I had to do battle with Susie, some reinforcement was necessary.

A large fruit block was in my pocket, and I demolished that before riding up to her. We exchanged a few words as I passed, and immediately I increased my pace. But the seconds went by without her appearing again, and at the next turn I realized that Susie was not challenging me.

At 100 miles I had caught the whole field.

The lads were in great form. Time after time they would cut across from one part of the course to another—either on their bikes or in the van—so as to be ready to hand up fruit drinks, chocolate, or grapes, or to pass me a sponge dipped in water and Eau de Cologne to refresh me when my face and neck became hot and dusty.

Refreshment for themselves they took as and when they could, and on at least one occasions their hard-earned break was cut short by my unexpectedly early arrival. The row of bicycles outside a village pub suggested that their owners thought there was plenty of time for a 'quick one' before I came through. But before they could down their pints, the cry went up—'She's here!' And they had to leave their glasses and dive for their bicycles, for fear of missing me at the next point.

More than one marshal, too, was caught napping in more sense than one. 'Am I going right?' I would call, and, startled, they would leap to their feet to reassure me in the nick of time. Then, as the significance of my arrival dawned on them, they would yell after me: 'Lash 'em down, lass; you're doing a flier!'

Eventually I reached the finishing circuit, with its two level crossings, nasty hills, and an acute bend

—and the organizers had to do some quick thinking. For I had completed the planned course of 223 miles, had broken the national competition record, and had still forty minutes left before my twelve hours were up.

An emergency course was hastily planned. I was sent on to the men's circuit in the reverse direction. This caused quite a stir all round, for my helpers had not realized that I should not be allowed to cover the women's circuit for a fourth time. When told, they lost no time in piling their bicycles into Laurie's van and setting off to find me. Meanwhile, pedalling happily along, I was greatly amused to see the surprised looks on the faces of riders in the men's event as I rode towards them.

The end of my twelfth hour approached, and a car was brought into service to follow me at a distance of 100 yards. An official told me to stop as soon as I heard three hoots. I put everything into that last half mile or so, and the final minutes seemed to creep by. Then suddenly there came a blare of horns, and, easing the pressure from my 79·7-inch fixed gear, I applied my brakes.

The '12-hour' was over; the race I had longed to ride. I thought I had done well; I knew that I had done my best. In that happy moment I wanted only one thing—and, looking beyond the official car, I was delighted to see 'our' little van. And there were Ken, and Laurie, and all the lads dashing up to congratulate me.

Immediately I had stopped riding it began to feel cold, so I was wrapped in a blanket, popped into the van, and taken back for a meal. The racing boys who had finished their '12', were enjoying their food when I arrived.

'What have you all done?' I asked. 'Not as well as you,' came the reply. And then they told me.

I had amassed 237·628 miles, beating the existing women's national record by almost seventeen miles. If I had been riding among the eighty men in the men's event, I should have been placed fifth. Their winner had covered barely six miles more.

The lads said they had never had a more exciting day in all their years of cycling. There were celebrations that night in Coventry . . .

With an average speed of 21·827 m.p.h. over three distances (25, 50, and 100 miles) I became, for that year, winner of the Women's British Best-All-Rounder Contest. In December 1949 I went on to the platform at the Empress Hall in London to receive my championship awards, to the generous applause of a huge audience of cycling folk, including of course my own clubmates, my husband Ken, and my son Clive—who did not quite understand it all, but was very thrilled all the same.

It was indeed a thrilling evening to round off an exciting racing year, but something more was to come—something that meant, and still means, a very great deal to me.

At the Coventry Cycling Club's annual dinner the following January I received a beautifully illuminated address which reads as follows:

AN APPRECIATION

Members and friends of the Coventry Cycling Club desire to place on record their admiration of the achievement of a fellow member

Eileen Sheridan.

Riding a bicycle in the Yorkshire Cycling Federation's women's open 12-hour road time trial on September 24, 1949, Mrs. Sheridan covered the distance of 237 miles, 5 furlongs, 97 yards, an accomplishment unprecedented by a woman on British roads. The honour attending her performance gives the utmost pleasure to her clubmates and friends everywhere.

January 1950 (Signed) HARRY WESTON
President

Later that night I was also asked to sign the *Golden Book of Cycling*—and so the name of Sheridan went down at the end of a distinguished list of others stretching back into cycling history—names which I had honoured and which I had never imagined would one day include my own.

That was indeed an evening I shall never forget.

CHAPTER NINE

Coveted Cycling Award is Mine

I now looked forward to even greater fitness.

My son Clive was growing fast, and was the proud owner of a tricycle which he manoeuvred with great skill. His antics would sometimes make me go cold. I had tried tricycle riding myself, but my efforts did not prove very successful. The ordinary cyclist, mounting a tricycle for the first time, can quite easily end up in a ditch, wondering how it happened!

George Herbert Stancer, O.B.E., who has probably done more for the sport and pastime of cycling than any man living, and who is known affectionately to many followers of the sport as 'Whiskers in the Wind', is still, at the age of 78, a very active cyclist and tricyclist. He is President of the Cyclists' Touring Club, the world's greatest cycling club and the organization that first introduced Ken and me to the good companionship of club cycling. It was therefore with special pleasure that I accepted an invitation to his home.

After dinner he said he wished to try an experiment, and I watched innocently while he brought a tricycle from his garage. He asked me and another lady guest (a non-cyclist) to ride the machine in turn.

The non-cyclist mounted and rode with no difficulty round the spacious drive. It looked so easy that I wasted no time when my turn came. 'Steady,' called out G. H. S. as I set off at a fair pace. And then I tried to turn.

The three-wheeled juggernaut continued in a straight line, and nothing I could do would make it behave otherwise. Squealing with horror, I disappeared into Mr Stancer's thick shrubbery. Emerging sheepishly, I realized I had provided the onlookers with considerable entertainment, as well as proving a theory to the satisfaction of the owner of the tricycle.

But one can forgive G. H. S. almost anything—and the incident certainly taught me a lesson. I have stuck to two wheels ever since.

* * * *

Excellent news for racing girls was announced in 1950 by the R.T.T.C.—the inauguration of a women's 100-mile championship. It seemed obvious that this would stimulate very keen competition, and so it proved.

The event was a battle right from the beginning. Usually a slow starter, I was lying fourth to Janet Gregory of the Nottingham Wheelers, Elsie Horton (Coventry Road Club), and Joyce Brooker (South-Eastern Road Club) at the 30-mile check. It gave me quite a shock when Ken called out that I was two minutes down on Janet, but not to worry.

Not worry! I was shaken. Quickening my pace, I

really settled down. The morning became hot, and I revelled in it. Between fifty and eighty miles I overtook first Elsie Horton and then Joyce Brooker, who had started ten minutes before me. Having eaten in the first fifty miles, I took only drinks in the second half of the ride.

The last nineteen and a half miles were into a breeze, and although Janet had slowed over the final stages she broke the national competition record by one minute. But I came in to take this short-lived triumph from her—my time of 4 hours, 37 minutes 53 seconds being over 5½ minutes inside the existing record. Elsie had had to retire at ninety-two miles, and the third girl, Mary Martin (Doncaster Wheelers) was 12 minutes away.

The next important event was the Championship '50' in which Janet was defending her title. At twenty-seven miles she led the field by 45 seconds, but again I managed to put in a strong finish to take the title and break the national competition record.

My average speed of 22·134 over three road distances (25, 50, and 100 miles) gained me the title of British Best All-rounder for the second successive year.

Several other victories followed in the shorter distances, but I had my eye once again on the 12-hour record. My aim was to equal or even better last year's performance, if only to convince the people—and there were not a few of them—who just would not believe that a girl could cover 237 miles in twelve hours.

Some had even said that I had cut out a part of the course, and one particularly assertive racing type was sure a mistake had been made in the calculations. I didn't argue; just told him to wait and see.

'Next year,' I promised, 'I shall go up to Yorkshire to repeat the performance.'

So I did—but what a day to pick! An unfavourable weather forecast proved only too correct, and it was fortunate I had taken the precaution of covering the whole of my body with olive oil to keep out the cold dampness. Twelve hours is a mighty long time to remain saturated.

Cold rain was lashing down at the start, and the sight of dark-clad figures disappearing at minute intervals into the gloom of the early morning was not encouraging. But I set my teeth, determined this time to ride hard all the way and not to take it easy at any point. I felt quite confident of being able to last a '12' even in those conditions.

Grins and nods were exchanged along the course with the men riding in the opposite direction, but as the day wore on it looked as though they were dropping out one by one.

At length I had caught all the girls except Mary Martin of Doncaster Wheelers who, having accidentally cut out two miles of the course, had gained that much ground on me. This fact had been discovered when Mary had failed to turn up at one check, but had appeared at the next. I learned about it with great relief; it explained why, although I had been cycling really strongly, there had been no sign of her.

At last I saw her in the distance, and, putting on speed, began to draw very gradually nearer. She looked round and, seeing me, increased her pace. It became a battle royal between the two of us. Relentlessly I pounded my pedals and drew level with her. For a while we rode neck-and-neck, fighting a very stiff headwind.

Surely she could not keep that killing pace for long. I looked at my watch. We had been riding for seven hours.

'Only five hours to go,' I murmured. There was a groan from Mary, and—surprisingly—I saw no more of her.

The club boys appeared like angels, feeding me and keeping me happy throughout the event. My father, who was with Ken this time, encouraged me at every possible point. As before, I completed the women's finishing circuit three times and ended up on the men's course. It was surprising how few finishers there were; half the men had packed it in.

Towards the end I myself was beginning to feel the effects of my battle against the elements. And when an official called out that my last year's distance would be equalled, I shook my head. Yet at the end of my twelve hours it was calculated that I had covered 236 miles—not much more than a mile less than the previous effort. And, with a clear win of fifteen miles over my nearest rival, I considered this to be definitely my best performance to date.

We had all decided to stay the night in Wetherby, so the first thing I did at the hotel was to jump into a hot bath. On returning to my bedroom I found Ken in bed and fast asleep, exhausted after tearing about for twelve hours looking after me. I left him and went downstairs to do justice to a delicious dinner.

* * * *

It was Mary Rawlinson's idea that I should make an attempt on one of the long-distance national place-to-place records. Mrs Rawlinson is secretary of the Women's Road Records Association, and, although she talked me into it, I didn't really need much persuasion. Once she had shown Ken how to make out an official schedule for such an attempt, it only remained to decide which record to begin with. We agreed on the Birmingham to London.

The rules of the W.R.R.A. are very strict. Any cyclist attempting a record should have an official observer from the Association to be in a following car with a specially appointed timekeeper. This car is not allowed to approach closer than 100 yards, unless the rider puts a foot to the ground.

One official car is allowed to pass the rider, and helpers use this to get ahead to marshal the course and feed the cyclist. The latter is not allowed to take pace from any vehicle or other rider, or to take food from helpers unless they are on foot.

Official starting points from most towns are the Head Post Offices, so it is necessary to start in the early hours of the morning in order to miss traffic congestion. It was five o'clock on a dark morning in October when I left the H.P.O. in New Street, Birmingham.

St Martin's Church was striking the hour, and the sound of the chimes echoed along empty streets which later would be bustling with hurrying crowds and heavy traffic. Over the cobbled Bull Ring I rode, and away into the country, where I jettisoned my lamps as soon as it became light. And, just through Coventry, my mother and father were at the roadside to wish me luck.

The police had been notified of my attempt, and as I neared Barnet a mobile police officer went ahead on a motor-bike to give warning of my approach to policemen stationed at all the traffic signals.

Light after light went green for me as I approached. Transverse traffic was halted, and car and lorry drivers craned out of windows to see what all the fuss was about. A local procession perhaps—or an urgent government dispatch, a fire, a foreign notability, maybe even the King . . .

How their eyes must have popped when they saw a little girl in black sweater and shorts go tearing by on a bicycle!

Some of the police officers, with stop watches in their hands, called out encouragement, and I felt extremely grateful to them for their kind and very sporting co-operation.

Wren's famous dome of St Paul's in London told me the end of the ride was near, and, at the main G.P.O. in the shadow of the cathedral, the time keeper announced the success of my first W.R.R.A. record attempt. I had broken the record (set up in the previous July) by 13 minutes in spite of an annoying cross-wind, having taken 5 hours 22 minutes.

A bath and a change were first in my thoughts, but I could see that I wasn't to be allowed to relax for long. My husband was already discussing with the helpers plans for my next place-to-place ride—the London to Oxford and back.

It is the custom for cyclists making attempts on 'out and back' records to finish with the London end before the traffic gets too heavy. This is done by commencing on the outskirts, riding to the turn at Hyde Park Corner, back through the starting point to the other turn (in this case Oxford H.P.O.), and thence back to the start again.

We stayed the night with Ken's people in Richmond, Surrey, before setting off to the outskirts of London. It was bitterly cold when I started at 4 a.m. on what Mary Rawlinson said was a nice little easy record. I reminded her of this untruth afterwards, but she was quite unrepentant.

'I had to get you going somehow, you know,' she said.

On this 'nice little easy' record you have to climb over the Chiltern Hills in both directions. But I reached Oxford without incident, and was delighted to see my old friend Honor Hoborough (Oxford City C.C.) marshalling me through the back streets to the H.P.O.

Honor had evidently been giving me a big 'build-up', for as I approached the main road for my return to London the policeman on point duty immediately stopped the traffic to let me through. Carried away by the moment, he was jumping for joy and shouting 'Good Luck' to me in a rich Oxfordshire *burr*. I thanked him gratefully.

Someone else was in Oxford to see me. It was Clive—what a lovely surprise to see him standing by the roadside with my mother and father! They had motored down from Coventry, and intended to follow the official car back to London.

The Chilterns loomed up, and I learned afterwards that mother had turned to father and said 'Of course, dear, they won't send her over that hill. I expect she will go round it.' I had no such fond hopes. I had been here before!

The hill came nearer, until eventually we began to ascend the beautifully wooded slopes of the Aston Rowant climb. A cross-wind had come up, and my feet were frozen.

I was only 30 seconds up on the record, and Ken and the helpers had some anxious moments. But I refused to think about failure, and began to put on pressure. Twenty miles to go!

At one point the people in the following cars were horrified to see a helper hand me a drink while I was travelling very fast. Though he ran really hard to lessen the impact, my hand hit the flask with such force that the contents shot out like a fountain right over my head.

Slight cramp began to affect my right thigh, which made it necessary to ease the pressure on that leg for a short time. Then I put everything I had into the finishing stretch, and covered the final seven miles in 16 minutes. The record was mine by over 10 minutes.

So much for record-breaking that year. It had become bitterly cold, and though I felt fit, Ken thought it best for me to wait until the following year before attempting anything more. There was also a very heavy social season ahead.

In February 1951 the journal *Cycling* had its

Diamond Jubilee celebrations at the Royal Albert Hall, London. What an unforgettable evening it was! The thousands of cyclists present were in jubilant mood, and everyone was bubbling over with high spirits.

During the magnificent concert, Italy's Fausto Coppi—probably the greatest cyclist in the world—appeared on his first visit to England and gave a demonstration. Rollers were set up on a slowly revolving stand so that everyone could see that master of the art of pedalling in action from every angle. Moving spotlights, continually changing colour, picked out his graceful figure, and the roars of applause from the audience showed their keen appreciation of the rare opportunity of seeing 'the maestro' in person.

To mark the occasion, *Cycling* presented some magnificent silver trophies to outstanding personalities of the racing game. I was honoured to find myself included with men like Reg Harris, Sid Patterson, and Ken Joy, and I was the only girl to receive an award.

Amid all the exciting memories of that great evening, it is surprising how a small incident has stuck. It was after the presentation, when the 'stars' were each asked to say a few words into the microphone and then take a seat on the platform. Wearing my favourite evening gown, a strapless affair, I took my place next to Alf Hill, the long-distance rider—a fact that did not pass unnoticed by one of the many amateur humorists in the audience.

'Mind out, Alf!' he called—and of course at that moment the great hall went suddenly quiet so that the remark came over very clearly. It raised a big laugh in the crowd and a deep flush on Alf's face (or perhaps it was the spotlights!)

At the end of that grand gala night everyone in the vast hall joined hands to sing Auld Lang Syne—an amazing sight as thousands of linked arms moved to and fro in unison, looking for all the world like huge waves. We had taken Clive with us, and it is hardly necessary to add that he loved every moment of it.

* * * *

Early in March I received a letter from the honorary secretary of the F. T. Bidlake Memorial Trust, stating that I had been awarded the Bidlake Memorial Plaque for 1950—'for creating a new high standard in women's cycle racing with an outstanding series of three championships and five record performances on the road in 1950'.

The Bidlake Plaque! Who would have imagined back in those early days with the club that in a few short years I should have come so far? The many struggles I had had along the road seemed all worth while, and I wanted only to do better still—in tribute to those other famous recipients of the Plaque of whose company I now was, and to the memory of Bidlake himself.

For more than forty years, until his tragic death in 1933, the name of Bidlake dominated the world of cycling. As a practical cyclist and an able administrator and advocate, there have been few to surpass him, and he held deservedly high office in the Cyclists' Touring Club, the Road Records Association, and the North Road Cycling Club. His dazzling victories on road and track—and particularly on a tricycle—were the talk of his day, and at one time he held the whole sequence of tricycle road records from 50 miles to 24 hours.

The Memorial Plaque was endowed for annual award for achievements in various fields of cycling, covering, as far as possible, all the interests with which Bidlake himself had been associated. It is presented for outstanding performances in competitions or record attempts on road or track; for legislative or administrative work for cycling; for writings or other meritorious publications; or for some outstanding advancement in design or technical development in cycle construction.

The Bidlake Plaque is one of my most treasured possessions, for it set the seal on my success as an amateur racing cyclist.

Any winner of this award is the guest at a special dinner held in his or her honour. Mine was held in Coventry on 9th June 1951. It was organized by my own club, and the chairman was our jovial club president, Councillor (now Alderman) Harry Weston, who by a happy chance was Mayor of Coventry that year. The dinner was attended by many of my friends and relatives, including my grandparents who had travelled up from London specially for the evening. My mother and father were very proud.

My grandfather, still a keen sportsman despite his eighty years, is as fit as a fiddle and enjoys a game of golf even to this day. He is the proud possessor of an enormous gold medal which he won for being first home in a race from London to York on bicycles, wearing full army kit.

But he insists that his greatest claim to fame is in simply being my grandfather. As he said at the dinner, if it hadn't been for him there would be no Eileen Sheridan.

CHAPTER TEN

My Hopes Materialize

Early in the year, in almost arctic conditions, I had started to train again. It was after one freezing ride that I found I had a pain in the small of my back. Strangely enough, it couldn't be felt when in racing position on the cycle, so I continued to train very seriously.

Gradually the pain went, and I seemed reasonably fit, but somehow my legs hadn't the necessary zip in them. When after intensive training my real racing form still eluded me, I began to think that something must be wrong. I was sure of it when, in a 50-mile event near Nottingham, I failed to gain a place. The following week end saw me again with the also-rans in another '50'—this time on the Bath Road.

During these two races my right leg felt decidedly 'heavy', so before riding in any more events I decided to visit a qualified masseur. Mr Fletcher of Coventry, whose skilled hands sought out the cause of all the trouble, diagnosed a slight inflammation of the sciatic nerve and set to work accordingly.

After a second visit I was declared 100% fit, so the following week end Ken and I were down on the Bath Road again ready for yet another 50-mile race. For although Mr Fletcher had assured me that he had completely dispelled the sciatic trouble, I was still anxious to know whether my right leg would stand up to the strain of pushing a high gear for over two hours.

My fears were groundless, however. Pounding along with all my former zest, I won the event in 2 hours 13 minutes—my fastest '50'—without any trouble.

The 50-mile championship for 1951 was to be run on the same course the following week-end, but something happened during the next few days to give me other things to think about.

From the Hercules Cycle & Motor Co. Ltd. I received a letter saying that they had followed my career with great interest, and asking if I would care to go along for an interview. Mrs Lyn Stancer, president of the Women's Road Records Association, accompanied me to Birmingham, where we met D. D. McLachlan, Hercules Director of Publicity.

He was ready with an offer. If I would consider turning professional, the Hercules Company would sign me up.

'What will it entail?' I asked.

'We shall want you to attack all the professional records for us.'

The professional road records! Records held at the time by Marguerite Wilson (who had also ridden for Hercules)—the same Marguerite Wilson whose autograph I had rather timidly sought at that Best-All-Rounder Concert back in 1945!

Here was an opportunity for which I had longed. As an amateur I could never have travelled all over the country attacking long-distance records. The expense would have been far too great, especially as I had a family to think about.

f

I did not hesitate. I signed up as a professional cyclist, and looked forward with great enthusiasm to my new career.

Although my professional racing was not to commence until 1952, I did not ride in the 50-mile championship as I had planned. My amateur career had finished the moment I signed for Hercules.

My debut before the public was at the 1951 Cycle Show at Earls Court, where I was in attendance on the Hercules Stand to sign autographs and answer questions. It was an exciting week, though very exhausting, as anyone who has completed a show week of any kind will agree. Amid the bright lights, the stuffy atmosphere, and the milling crowds of over-enthusiastic autograph-hunters, there were times when I longed for the open country and the road in front of me. I was well and truly fatigued at the end of each long day.

One became used to hearing comments—but there were times when self-control was difficult. I well remember, for instance, two cockney boys who pushed to the front of the crowd, one declaring in a loud voice—'Oi, that's Eileen Sheridan!'

'Don't be daft,' the other replied, eyeing me up and down in a decidedly unpleasant way. 'She couldn't push a bike to save 'er life!' The urge to hurry their exit was almost irresistible.

An amusing interlude was a meeting with Ronald Shiner for the purpose of appearing in a film 'short'. My role was to show him how to mount and ride a bicycle. Those who have seen Ronald on stage or screen can imagine the tangle he managed to get into.

It was my pleasure also to be introduced to

'Stainless Stephen' (otherwise A. C. Baynes), who made a big name as a radio entertainer between the wars. What is less well known is that he is an accomplished and very enthusiastic cyclist. A member of the famous North Road Club, as well as the Cyclists' Touring Club, Stainless has ridden in a 24-hour event, which he described characteristically as 'semi-colon, semi-conscious, full stop'! He is still a keen cycle tourist, and his ready wit is often heard in cycling company.

I remember being with a crowd in a very hot room, where almost everyone looked very red in the face. Only G. Herbert Stancer, the C.T.C. president whom I have spoken of earlier, seemed to be unaffected by the heat. Out flashed a typical 'Stainless' comment:

'I say, George, you've forgotten to put your make-up on!'

Show Week came to an end, and now I had to settle down to serious training. It was my intention to cover as many miles as possible to prepare myself for the long-distance record attempts.

My parents suggested that we sell our house and take over half of theirs, so that, on the many occasions when I would be away, Ken and Clive would be well looked after. This we agreed to do. Clive adored his grandparents, and it made me very happy to know that my family would be in such good hands.

I was riding hard one day along the Coventry-London road near Towcester when it happened.

Brilliant sunshine, alternating with deep shadows cast across the road by the trees, must have prevented me from seeing a large wooden chock left in the road by some unthinking lorry driver. My front wheel hit it, and I was thrown right over the handlebar. At least, so I was told afterwards—for my head met the ground with such force that I was knocked unconscious immediately, and my memory of the accident is very vague.

It happened so suddenly that I was completely relaxed on falling, which no doubt saved my bones from being broken. Nevertheless my forehead received a nasty gash that bled very badly. Fortunately the whole incident was seen by a 'good Samaritan', in the guise of another lorry driver, who pulled up, covered me with his coat, and asked a passing motorist to summon the police and an ambulance.

The latter had to come from the Northampton General Hospital, some nine miles away, and I had lost a considerable amount of blood by the time it arrived. While being moved into the ambulance, I recovered consciousness slightly, and I can vaguely remember saying, in a voice that didn't sound at all like my own, 'Please don't leave me'.

'Don't you worry, dear, we won't leave you,' came the gruff reply . . . and I knew no more until I came-to again in Northampton Hospital to find Ken and my father at the bedside.

My cycle had been taken to Towcester police station, where luckily it was recognized by one of the office staff, who contacted my family immediately. Ken and father had dashed from Coventry by car, but I was feeling too ill to realize any of this. In fact, I imagined myself in Coventry Hospital, and was under that impression until two days after the accident.

The wound in my head required twelve stitches just across the right temple, and I suffered extreme giddiness for a long while afterwards. Every time I turned on to my left side in bed, I had a most dreadful sensation of falling. Even to-day, when overtired, I have to be very careful if I put my head back or stretch up to reach anything.

When I was well enough to take an interest in things, my nurse made me laugh as she described her astonishment when she came to undress me after I was brought in. Under my training suit she had found a thick continental sweater, under that another—and another, and yet another, until there were five in all. I pointed out that for training purposes in our climate, and especially in the early mornings, it was necessary to put on a little extra clothing to get really warmed up.

'A little extra!' It was her turn to laugh.

Many friends from Northampton cycling clubs visited me, and after three weeks I went to London to spend a quiet Christmas with Ken's family. Then, back in Coventry, I started once again to build up my fitness for the 1952 season.

The Hercules Company arranged for Frank Southall to manage my record attempts. Frank had been the greatest record-breaker of his time: unbeatable when on peak form. Frank knew what was ahead of me. He was experienced in the game, and I had great faith in him.

He had never seen me ride, but my times proved my ability to endure long-distance cycling. He decided that, as my first professional ride, I should tackle the London to Portsmouth and back record—

a mere 138 miles, but a tough road which would help prepare me for the longer distances.

I stayed with Ken's family in Richmond, and at one o'clock in the morning a car drove up to take me to the start at Esher. My bicycles were strapped on to a special stand at the back of the car.

At the wheel was Monty Southall (Frank's brother), and I little realized just then how many miles Monty would eventually cover, driving behind me at the regulation 100 yards. He became a part of all my records, and I always felt heartened to know that, after setting me off at the time-keeper's word, he would climb into his car with the other officials and be 'right behind me' all the way. Like his brother, Monty was a big barrel-chested man who was always ready with a joke when the tension was greatest.

At Esher I had expected to find just the timekeeper, my manager, the official observer, and a few helpers. Instead there was a long line of cars and quite a crowd of people, despite the unearthly hour. Newspapermen strode forward to interview me; photographers edged round seeking vantage points and fiddling with flashbulbs.

I gaped stupidly for a moment; then I wanted to run. Finally I stood and talked. It was no use sighing for the old days; I was a professional cyclist now, and this sort of thing was part of the business. As time went on, I learned to accept it as 'all in the day's work'.

The morning was very cold, and I was pushed off at 2 a.m., which is in my opinion the worst possible time to have to be wide awake; it just isn't natural.

However, there was the usual worry to finish with the London end first because of traffic congestion.

I set off fast, riding towards the capital—but in Putney I lost my way. The roads looked so different in the darkness. The faithful Monty, immediately realizing the situation, hooted to make me look back, and at the same time showed me with his car indicator which way to turn. It was all over in a few moments—but on a ride like this every few moments were precious.

Having turned at Hyde Park Corner, I headed for Portsmouth. But it wasn't until London was left right behind that I realized just how bitterly cold it was that morning. Clad in a short-sleeved sweater and shorts, I began to long for one of the sweaters the nurse had peeled off me in Northampton Hospital.

The Portsmouth road is notorious for its chilly white mists, and I was soon in a swirling gloom—my small lamps useless. And the car headlamps, which had been picking up the cat's-eyes in the road, were now of no help to me.

The freezing air began to get into me. My muscles became numbed. My speed dropped. I had asked for cold drinks (though my manager had suggested hot), but now the fruit drink in the bottle on the front of the bike went down my throat like iced-water as I sucked it up through a tube. My chest tightened, and it felt as if someone were squeezing my lungs so that they could not be filled with air. Breathing became difficult, but as high a speed as possible was kept up through the quiet villages and little country towns.

Hindhead was climbed as dawn was breaking, and

I thought it a beautiful sight despite my labouring.

At Portsmouth G.P.O. the return journey began, and at the top of Portsdown Hill I would have given anything to have stopped cycling. But to fail on this, my very first professional attempt, would be dreadful.

Someone offered me another drink, but I refused it because my bottle of cold liquid was still over half full. What I had not yet realized was that my most urgent need was for a strong hot drink to give my body a chance to warm up.

'It's a long way back to London, you know,' the helper called, but I rode on regardless.

Hindhead was reached again—and there was Ken, my husband, looking anxiously at his watch. I was five minutes down on Marguerite Wilson's time for the distance.

'Give it all you've got! I know you can do it,' called Ken.

But by this time my breathing had become really laboured. I was gasping for air. For all Ken's confidence in me, I do not think I could have carried on had not Frank Southall, my manager, handed me a hot drink.

'Drink it all, kid, and don't worry,' he yelled, and this time I did as I was told. The hot liquid warmed my whole body and enabled me to ride hard to the finish—just two minutes inside the record.

Bending over my handlebar to regain my breath, I was horrified to find I was coughing up small quantities of blood.

Frank at once arranged for me to see Sir Adolphe Abrahams, the eminent sporting specialist, and I reached the depths of despair as I awaited his verdict. Had I injured my lungs? Was my career to end before it had properly begun? With great relief I learned that in fact a small bloodvessel in my throat had been broken through breathing hard in the icy air. It was nothing that would stop me cycling. Sir Adolphe advised making our starts a little later, and whenever possible this was arranged.

Frank wondered how my fitness compared with that of my amateur days, so the following week the schedules went in for the professional London to Oxford and back run. The amateur record was already mine, captured when I had been very fit indeed.

The start had again to be made at a very early hour, and once more my throat gave me trouble. My time was better than anyone else had done over that undulating road, but it was twelve minutes slower than my amateur figures. My disappointment was intense, and my confidence shaken. I no longer felt sure of my capabilities.

'There's only one answer to that,' said Frank Southall firmly. 'Ride. Ride until you find your old form again.'

In exactly three days I was attempting the Birmingham to London record. And this time, although the final thirty miles were fought into a really strong headwind, I did beat my amateur ride by two minutes, as well as bettering Marguerite Wilson's professional record by 25½ minutes.

Frank was there as I stepped off my cycle, and his expression told me that he was satisfied. I was satisfied too. At last I felt I had a grip on things again.

A film unit came out for my next ride—the 100-mile record on the Norwich road. Shots were taken at the start, at a feeding point along the route, and of what turned out to be a fighting finish. The scenes were included in the film 'Spinning Wheels' which was produced by the Dunlop Rubber Co. Ltd. and shown for the first time at the Earls Court Cycle Show later in the year. This production proved very popular, and was subsequently shown at club social functions all over the country.

One incident, at the 50-mile mark, could have turned that film into a 'funnie'. My manager, handing me up a drink, rather underestimated my speed, with the result that when I took it the liquid splashed out all over my face and hair. The drink had been well sugared, and as it dried on me my skin became taut and my eyelashes stuck together when I blinked. At the end of the ride, my hair was well and truly set by the drink into wind-blown waves and curls.

'What on earth must I look like?' I gasped, trying vainly to tug a comb through it.

Frank Southall only laughed. 'You look fine,' he replied. 'Eileen the Glamour Girl—and all thanks to the Southall Patent Setting Lotion!'

So June ended with my recording 4 hours 16 minutes 1 second for the 100 miles, beating the existing professional figures by fifteen minutes.

First on the list in July was the Liverpool to London record, a ride of 201 miles. I enjoyed the opportunity to look round Liverpool with its fine buildings and glorious modern cathedral, and to pass through the Mersey Tunnel in the car for the first time was a wonderful experience.

Liverpool club folk turned out to marshal me through the city as the ride began, but a feeling of extreme loneliness overcame me as I plunged into the Mersey Tunnel—devoid at that early hour of its usual continuous stream of noisy traffic.

Emerging from the tunnel, I realized the wind was against me. I fought into it, but a group of cycling clubmen whom I passed shook their heads very gloomily.

'You've got the wrong wind, Eileen,' they said, and—as the modern jargon has it—I couldn't have agreed more! I continued to try hard, however, telling myself that conditions could change. They did—for the worse. The wind gained in force until terrific gusts were hitting me—now head-on, now striking across. It was extremely difficult even to hold the cycle on the road.

On Meriden Hill, near the centre of England, my manager stood waiting, and I quite expected him to stop me. But all the helpers yelled out 'You've got a chance; keep it going!' Keep it going! Easy to say—but try doing it with a gale buffeting your cycle from all sides.

Whenever my rides took me through Coventry, my father would be at the roadside to cheer me on, but to-day I looked for him in vain. From his window he had seen how the wind was blowing, imagined that a start would not have been made, and gone back to bed.

It would have paid us all to have done the same—for I battled on down that long road only to be stopped at Dunstable, five minutes down on Marguerite's record. With only thirty-three miles to go, and no chance of a change in the weather, my prospects were hopeless.

Try again! The following week-end saw us off to Liverpool once more, but the weather forecast was the same as for the previous occasion. There was a great deal of discussion about whether the attempt should be made; we didn't want another failure.

The timekeeper, the late B. W. Best, seemed against starting, and that almost decided it. But as we were moving away Frank asked if I would like to take a chance.

'If it's as bad as last week, we won't let you ride on so far,' he assured me hastily. 'What do you say, Eileen?'

'All right,' I said, 'I'll try.'

My feelings were very mixed as I set about a task that appeared impossible, but you can never tell with our weather. After about thirty miles the wind gradually dropped and the sun came out. It became very warm, and later a slight breeze sprang up in my favour. I couldn't believe my luck.

This time I waved gaily to my father as I sped through Coventry, and the local police wished me luck. On through quaint old Dunchurch, Towcester, and the Stratfords, boys and girls from the cycling clubs were out at points all along the route. Then came Dunstable, St Albans, and the long run into London.

At a very busy road crossing, one of my helpers, seeing a troop of Boy Scouts nearby, went over and asked if they would like to do their good turn for the day. By joining hands and holding up the traffic should the lights be against me, he explained, they might make all the difference to my chances. The Scouts jumped at the idea. The lights did show red as I came bowling along, and they spread themselves in a line over the road, effectively preventing anything from cutting across my path.

Unfortunately the very first vehicle to come up against the Scout barrier was a police car! My helper had a busy session of explanations and apologies, but the police were most understanding and sportingly overlooked the whole episode.

Four cars containing helpers and officials were following me on this ride, and—believe it or not—one by one they all fell by the wayside with some trouble or other. The last to break down, that carrying the timekeeper and observer, did so when I was within six miles of the finish. Had I punctured then, my position would have been pretty desperate. But quite unaware that I was alone, and oblivious of the panic behind me, I pedalled along merrily.

Meanwhile the occupants of the official car had jumped out and waved frantically at the first car to come along. By a great stroke of good fortune the driver happened to be the Hercules London Manager who had decided to come out to see me on the final stretch, not realizing what an important part he was to play in the event.

One of my spare tyres was taken from the abandoned car, and everyone piled into the London Manager's vehicle. Soon I was caught again, and my progress anxiously watched over the remaining miles of busy traffic and cobbled surfaces. But the bike held out better than the cars, and, with no punctures or other breakdowns, I romped up to the G.P.O. in

London 9 hours 39 minutes after leaving Liverpool and 23 minutes better than the existing time for the ride.

Yes, a good deal of luck, as well as hard work, is required for record-breaking.

* * * *

The Liverpool to Edinburgh record was next on my list, so early in August we were back again in the Merseyside port.

Frank Sleman, one of Liverpool's foremost cycling officials, agreed to help us with marshals and feeders for the first 100 miles. But on studying the schedule he gasped at the amount by which I was expected to beat the record. It was more than an hour.

I, too, had queried Frank Southall's figures, imagining that he had not allowed for my slowing up on the two long ascents of Shap and Devil's Beef Tub —both over 1300 feet.

My manager was quite unperturbed. 'It may look a bit stiff to you,' he told the Liverpool Frank, 'but I tell you she'll do it.'

All went well in the early stages, but I wondered what speed I could maintain on the hard climbs ahead. The scenery on Shap and Devil's Beef Tub was more impressive than any I had raced through before—and so were the ascents. I fought strongly up the long winding road to the summits, fortified by the knowledge that 'what goes up must come down.'

Sure enough the exhilarating swoops from the high ground amply compensated for the gruelling climbs, and I was told afterwards that my speed on those descents was over 30 m.p.h. for miles on end.

Approaching Edinburgh, Frank called out that I was equalling his own pre-war record and, as he put it, 'busting my schedule wide open'.

The Scottish capital, preparing for its world-famous music festival the following week, was absolutely crowded. It was a tricky job to negotiate the rough cobbles, and officials in the following car said they were given some nasty moments as I nipped about among the people, tramlines, trams, and dogs.

At the side of the Head Post Office I pulled up and looked for Mr Best. There was a frantic moment, for he was not there.

'Where the blazes is the timekeeper?' I burst out as my manager came rushing across the road to me.

His reply was brief. 'Quick, kid, run with your machine to the corner.' This I did, and there, fifty yards further on, standing, watch in hand, quietly and unobtrusively among the milling crowd, was B. W. Best. It was the north-west corner of the post office that was the official terminal point.

Feeling very fit and looking fresh after a shower and a change of clothing, I went into the hotel lounge where a newspaper reporter was waiting to interview me. His first question was 'When are you starting this ride from Edinburgh to Liverpool?'

'It's the other way round,' I replied, 'and I've just finished it.' He was quite speechless.

Frank Southall's schedule had indeed been miscalculated, but not, as I had imagined, over-optimistically. My time of 10 hours 8 minutes 20 seconds was more than two hours faster than the existing record, and better by a few minutes than

Frank's pre-war figures over the same route. He was delighted by my success, and seemed as pleased as though he had done the ride himself.

Thick white mist persisted when, towards the end of August, the London to Bath and back was attempted. I was really cold for at least half the journey. And in the very early morning hours an enormous white owl swooped out of the darkness as if to attack me. Twice—three times—it came back, and I ducked my head as it dive-bombed. It was a strange and rather terrifying experience, and I rode hard to get away from the creature's hunting-ground as soon as possible.

On the return ride to London I was doubled-up with tummy-ache, and had to make several stops. As soon as I had passed the timekeeper, Frank rushed me back to the hotel.

'Eat any fruit yesterday?' he rapped.

'Grapes,' I confessed.

'How many?'

I told him. Grapes are my favourite fruit. I had bought a pound and eaten the lot.

'Skins as well?' Frank pressed, relentless.

I nodded.

'Well, my girl, let that be a lesson to you.'

It certainly was. But even so I had managed to break the record by 9 minutes.

Next came a very severe trial indeed. I had never cycled for more than twelve hours at any time, and the Land's End to London route—a matter of 287 miles—would really put my staying powers to the test.

The attempt was made early in October 1952,

and it proved to me just how tough the long-distance cycling game could be. For the first time in my life I was assailed by fatigue, intense and overpowering. My eyelids felt leaden, and I fought a hard battle against the desire to fall asleep while still pedalling.

My speed dropped in the darkness, and occasionally I actually dozed off, to come to with a shock when I became conscious of the headlamps of some vehicle coming towards me. Monty Southall and the officials said it was painful to watch me.

As soon as the lights of Staines appeared, my spirits rose, and my speed increased to over 20 m.p.h. I finished at Hyde Park Corner exactly 23 minutes 13 seconds inside the record, having been in the saddle for 16 hours, 45 minutes, 47 seconds.

That ride taught me a great deal. I had been taking egg and milk drinks, and the amount consumed on the long journey upset my digestion and greatly affected my cycling towards the end. Frank, my manager, decided we would try a different method of feeding for future records.

As I climbed from my cycle I was handed a box containing a gay green-and-white bobbled woollen hat, of the type I had admired on some French sailors at Penzance.

'They're cute, aren't they?' I had said (meaning the hats). 'What a pity I haven't time to stop and buy one.'

I had thought no more about it, but someone had. A hotel porter had been despatched to buy one of the hats as soon as the shops were open and to put it on a train for London. And Mr G. W. H. Gibbs, Hercules advertising agent, had put in a long-distance call from Cornwall to his office, instructing one of his staff to meet the train and bring the precious parcel to Hyde Park Corner for presentation to me at the finish.

I had no idea of all the trouble that had been taken, but it was a lovely surprise, and—as Mr Gibbs pointed out afterwards—probably the most expensive hat I have ever worn!

But there was another sort of surprise awaiting me. I had already been rather puzzled during the ride to see people at their cottage doors to wish me luck, or assembled at various points in the towns to see me go by. Out in the country farm workers had waved from their carts or tractors, or given me a cheer from the fields.

As I have explained before, these record attempts are strictly 'hush-hush', no advance publicity being allowed, and the only people who wave to me as a rule are friends and helpers, newspapermen or police, who have been supplied in confidence with advance details. The small doubts that had been crossing my mind during the ride grew into a big one as a crowd of about 500 people gave me a rousing welcome at the finish. *How did these people know?*

It was not long before I knew the worst. That very morning one of the national daily papers had broken faith and printed information about the route—including the approximate time of my arrival at Hyde Park Corner.

Rule 44 of the Women's Road Records Association had been broken, and, in spite of the fact that the notice in the Press was no fault of mine, my claim to the arduous Land's End to London record was disallowed. My feelings can be imagined, for it meant that I should have to go through the whole thing again.

* * * *

One of the most miserable and uncomfortable of all these record rides was probably my first attempt on the London to York route. Starting off at 4 a.m. in pitch blackness and pouring rain, I had a few narrow squeaks on the slippery roads in London before getting out into the country.

Here, without street lamps to guide me, I was entirely dependent on the headlamps of Monty Southall's car, and often along the twisting lanes leading to the Great North Road I would round a bend to find myself in complete darkness in the lashing rain—my own lamp being quite inadequate in such conditions. Once, at a nasty bend, a helper called out to me to bear right. His timely warning saved me from heading straight for a brick wall.

As dawn broke, the usually lovely English countryside looked horribly grey, dismal, and oh so wet. A car drawing a horsebox went by, and a youth, leaning from a door at the back, called out to me, 'Are you enjoying yourself?'

'Fine,' I replied.

'How far as you going?'

'To York.'

The youth laughed a disbelieving laugh, and the vehicle sped on and disappeared from my sight.

After seven hours' riding, with a cold east wind cutting across the course and rain falling non-stop, I was frozen.

A stop to put on dry gloves was necessary to prevent my fingers from becoming totally numb.

At nine hours I was amused to notice the horsebox drawing level with me again. Evidently the driver had stopped for lunch somewhere *en route*. It was still raining, and I was still pedalling.

The youth's eyes goggled. 'Aren't you tired?' he called.

'No,' I replied. 'I love it.'

'Are you really going to York?'

'I hope so,' I muttered as raindrops dripped off the end of my nose.

'What on earth are you doing it for?'

I could stand no more of this, so glaring at him viciously, I said, 'If you must know, it's for "dollar lolly".' At this the youth disappeared inside, the car accelerated, and that was the last I saw of my tormentor.

Negotiating Doncaster was a really tricky job, and at one point Frank found he had held up a police car to let me through. It was in this city that my manager had left G. W. H. Gibbs with a hot drink for me. Now Mr Gibbs, as I have mentioned before, is from the agency that deals with Hercules advertising. But although his reason for coming was to obtain first-hand material for publicity purposes, he nevertheless insisted also on doing his share of marshalling and feeding.

When I reached the corner at which 'Gibby' was stationed, he looked a very sorry sight. With no shelter from the bitter wind and lashing rain, he had been standing there for half an hour, clutching my feeding-bottle to him to keep it warm, and holding the lapels of his suit to his neck, while water poured off his trilby in a gushing stream.

After Doncaster the wind hit me head-on. Time was getting short, the cold rain was beginning to affect me—and to make matters worse two level crossings were closed against me. Frank told me that by doing 20 m.p.h. to the finish I might just get the record.

It was a hard fight, and I passed B. W. Best, the timekeeper, at York H.P.O., with only two minutes to spare after ten hours' non-stop cycling. Having given me my time, Mr Best told me that Frank Southall was just round the corner expecting me to carry on for the 12-hour record, as I had two hours left in which to cover thirty-one miles.

The traffic in York was very heavy, and there were long queues of stationary cars held up by the lights. As I rode slowly up my inside lane, a girl on an enormous loop-framed bicycle suddenly cut across from between two cars in order to enter a side turning. I hit her machine amidships, and she merely put her foot to the ground to steady herself. But to my light racing bike the impact was like hitting a tank, and I fell in a heap on the road.

The curious stares of passers-by were a sure indication of my sadly bedraggled appearance as I replaced my unshipped chain and straightened my handlebar.

'Frank!' I shouted, and I looked appealingly at my manager as he appeared from round the corner. My body ached from the crash, and the cold rain was making me feel pretty grim. How I longed for a few words of sympathy! 'I've fallen off' I said in a tiny voice, 'and the cold is getting me down.'

'Never mind,' came the reply (in the typical Southall manner), 'you'll be all right.' And knew I had got to go on.

I consoled myself with the thought that the worst was over. Vain hope! A few miles on I was horrified to see a bull careering down the road ahead of me, with three men trying to manoeuvre it into a gateway. That was the last straw, and my immediate instinct was to turn my cycle round and ride hell-for-leather in the opposite direction.

'Carry on, Eileen; it's only a cow.' The cry came from Monty Southall behind me, and I hesitated. Then I slowly carried on, and was relieved to see the beast (quite definitely a bull) trot into the farm gateway.

Even that was not the end. A badly-placed sign-post caused me to go off course, and, with only thirty minutes of the twelve hours left, it was touch-and-go whether I should manage the record. I was really all-in when the timekeeper called me to a halt with 231 miles to my credit, just one mile better than the previous distance.

Back in York, still in a deplorable state and soaked to the skin, I felt slightly embarrassed walking into our smart hotel. The lift boy didn't turn a hair, but during dinner in the evening the waiter asked if I felt better after my fall into the river! He had seen me arrive, and thought I had just been dragged out.

It was getting rather late in the year for record-breaking, but off we went to stay at Penzance for a few days, hoping the wind would veer to the south-west for a last-minute attempt on the Land's End to London ride which (as explained earlier) I had to do again.

We had no luck at all. The wind stayed north, north, north. Then Frank Southall had a telephone call from Hercules in Birmingham, asking if we could start the next day. They wanted us back in London for the opening of the cycle show at Earl's Court.

I was against starting. The wind was against me, and, although it wasn't too cold in Cornwall, we knew there were thick frosts in the country. But as there was no question of waiting any longer, there was only one thing to do: make a start and see what happened.

From Land's End to Redruth and on to the Bodmin Moor climb, it was a battle all the way. A road sweeper leaning on his broom called out as I passed—'You've got the wrong wind, girl.' He didn't know how right he was.

Far down on my schedule, frozen to the marrow, I looked ahead and saw Frank waiting. I had little doubt of the decision my manager would make. As I approached, he stood in the road with outstretched arms. The ride was abandoned.

CHAPTER ELEVEN

We Move South

We returned to London in time for the opening, by His Royal Highness the Duke of Edinburgh, of the 1952 Cycle Show.

The Duke's great interest in sport and physical recreation is well known, and I was greatly honoured to be one of the cyclists presented to him. To us fell the opportunity to tell him just a little about the sport which we regard as the grandest of all.

His wonderful way of putting people at their ease soon dispelled the nervousness I had felt before he spoke to me. After chatting to me about my records, he asked if I ever cycled just for pleasure.

How I longed to tell him of the fun of it all, of the companionship in the clubs, of the wonderful spirit of those who turned out to ride or just to help in the darkness of the early morning and often in the rain. But of course there was only time for me to say Yes, cycling was always a pleasure to me and I actually enjoyed racing. The Duke seemed amused at my bubbling enthusiasm, and I often wonder if he really believed me.

That week was a particularly busy time for me. It involved introductions to many hundreds of people, numerous press interviews, and cross-questioning by large numbers of keen cyclists. By the end of the show the lack of fresh air had had its usual fatiguing effect on me.

All that winter strict training in the gym kept me fit in preparation for an even harder year, but I looked forward to the coming season with great enthusiasm.

As most of the W.R.R.A. records are based on London, it became inconvenient for me to have to keep travelling from Coventry, so Ken suggested we should look for a house in the south.

A likely-looking advertisement led us to the little village of Old Isleworth right on the river Thames, opposite Richmond Deer Park and Kew Gardens. The house was old property which had been modernized, and it was a case of love at first sight. We moved in just before Christmas 1952.

But in January, after a visit to Coventry for our club's annual dinner, we were dismayed to find that an exceptionally high tide over the week-end had, in our absence, flooded our new home to a depth of three inches.

Luckily we have tiled floors throughout on ground level, and, had we been at home to remove the carpets, we shouldn't have been bothered at all, for the water was completely free from mud and dirt. Fires, kept burning all day, soon dried out the carpets, and in next to no time we were back to normal again with no damage done.

The flooding would never had happened had the wall at the end of our garden been completed—and needless to say this job was now our first concern. There have been many very high tides since then, and we have suffered no further inconvenience. Yet after our first summer in Old Isleworth I told my husband that, even if we were to be flooded out every year, I should never want to leave this enchanting little spot.

The village, with its tall quaint Georgian houses and its ancient church, has a truly old-world atmosphere about it. Right on the river bank a famous old inn, the 'London Apprentice', overlooks scenes of activity that never fail to fascinate me. Fussy little tugs, barges, and even small cargo boats—ships of about 300 tons from Belgium, Holland, and Germany—pass the end of the garden on their way to some small wharves upstream.

For a boy a home like this is a paradise, and to Clive the river is a constant source of interest. When the captain of one of the cargo boats allowed him on board for tea with the crew, his excitement knew no bounds. Little wonder that Clive's bedroom has a distinctly nautical motif, with yachts decorating his curtains and model ships on his shelves.

We overlook the end of a small island known as Isleworth Ait, whose firm beach is a haunt of anglers at low tide. The scene is transformed by the rising tide, for it is then that the ducks and swans come clustering to be fed at our garden wall.

The river is never dull; there is activity all the year round. We have watched water-skiing from the garden in summer, and in the winter have fed the wheeling gulls from the same spot.

As many as sixteen herons have been counted standing in the water along Syon Reach awaiting the chance to snap up any unwary fish with their rapier-like beaks. During the pheasants' mating season their harsh screeching from the Ait is heard, and sometimes in the crisp early mornings we have watched from our bedroom windows the brilliantly plumed cock pheasants strut along our low wall—a lovely sight.

One day when Ken and I were paddling our kayaks along Syon Reach we were surprised to see three cormorants disporting themselves in the water just ahead of us. These birds are unprepossessing in appearance, but their ability to swim under water, to float like ducks, to walk on land, and to fly, puts them among the most versatile creatures on earth.

By far the most interesting and unusual visitor to our neighbourhood, however, was Sammy the Seal. The last time a seal had ventured so far up-river was over twenty-five years ago—and, sad to say, he came to an untimely end when, trapped under water by the lock gates at Richmond, he was drowned.

Sammy was first spotted one day at Isleworth in August 1953, and became quite a usual sight in the water near the Ait—to the great excitement of passers-by on the towpath. The news would spread like wildfire, and soon large crowds would gather to watch his antics.

He was a most inquisitive little chap, and every time a craft passed by he would pop up to find out exactly what was going on. On one occasion his bewhiskered face appeared only a few feet from my kayak. With big velvety eyes he regarded me for a moment; then in a trice he was gone.

Sammy stayed in the vicinity for about four months before making for the sea again.

* * * *

It was about this time that the *Daily Express* invited me on to the panel of a Sports Forum in Coventry. Sprinter McDonald Bailey and boxer Freddie Mills were among the other members of the panel gathered on the stage at the Central Hall.

I suppose I was fair game for the sort of question one member of the audience asked. He considered it wrong for women to participate in sport, particularly professionally. Women's place, he said, was in the home at the kitchen sink.

Asked to reply first, I said that women all over the world had performed admirably at most sports without losing their femininity, and were a great credit to their sex. The rest of the panel agreed with me wholeheartedly, but Freddie Mills couldn't resist pulling my leg about it afterwards when the panel relaxed behind the scenes. I playfully punched him on his huge chest, whereupon he doubled up, coughed loudly; then holding a large fist to the 'damaged' area, exclaimed 'I'm all in favour of women taking up boxing!'

I take my full share of the 'kitchen sink' part of life, and the newspapers love to photograph me washing-up. In addition to my nickname 'The Pocket Hercules' I have often been given headlines such as 'The cycling housewife', 'Cycling mother breaks record', etc.

Cycling is wonderful, but so is the happiness of family life. Our home is called 'The Anchorage', and I always return there with eagerness after my travels.

* * * *

Frank Southall had by this time collected a group

of helpers who knew the game inside out and upon whom he could depend unfailingly. From them I could receive accurate time checks and information about the road ahead.

With the party who set off for Scotland at the start of the 1953 season was Ken Joy, British Best All-Rounder for four years in succession and now signed on by the Hercules Company to attack the men's road records. After a spot of training with him to get acclimatized, I was all set for my attempt on the Edinburgh to Glasgow and back record.

The morning of 6th May was pleasant and sunny, and, having finished the Edinburgh end first, I was soon heading for Glasgow. My manager had shown me the route into Glasgow on the previous day, but now it was dreadfully busy and somehow in the heavy traffic I turned off between two marshals and became completely lost. When I failed to arrive at the Head Post Office, officials and helpers set off to search—and so we all spent quite a lot of valuable time running round Glasgow looking for one another.

At length it was all sorted out, and with relief I left the busy streets behind—to finish the ride with pleasure as I discovered that, despite the loss of time, I was 14½ minutes better than the previous best.

Edinburgh is one of my favourite cities, and while training there I made a point of visiting several of its historical places, including of course the magnificent castle.

But on 5th June it was good-bye to the Scottish capital, for that day Ken Joy and I were both attempting the Edinburgh to York run.

'See you in York!' I called to him as he was pushed off. And then it was my turn.

The wind was behind us at first, and the climbs over Soutra (1000 feet) and Carter Bar (1300 feet) were not too bad. But soon afterwards the wind veered, and on the flat finishing roads we both found it miserably cold and very hard.

Not far from Darlington some level crossing gates closed just as I reached them, and I had the vexing experience of having to wait until a goods train, which seemed to me to be about two miles long, struggled into view and clattered slowly past. I turned to the following car and shrugged my shoulders helplessly. The timekeeper got out to ask if I would like a cup of coffee, walked back, poured one out and brought it to me. And still the interminable train rattled on. It was six minutes before I could get away.

Nevertheless, both Ken Joy and I were successful, and it was interesting to compare experiences when we met again in York.

* * * *

That week had seen the Coronation of H.M. Queen Elizabeth II. During the celebrations that followed I was asked, together with that wonderful star of the stage and screen, A. E. Matthews, to open the Coronation Shopping Week at Ruislip in Middlesex.

The ceremony was to be held on the steps of a large cinema, but at the appointed time 'Mattie' hadn't turned up. It fell to me to give the opening speech, but my nervousness was soon dispelled by the warm welcome given me by the crowd.

Afterwards I was driven round Ruislip to see the modern shopping centre, and then on to a delightful roadhouse. With my hosts from the Council, I was enjoying a little appetizer before lunch when in walked Mr Matthews. He sat next to me, began chatting merrily with everyone, and soon seemed thoroughly at home. Seizing his opportunity, however, he suddenly whispered in my ear 'I say, my dear, can you tell me what this is all about?'

How I laughed! Playing up to him, I explained patiently that he was supposed to have helped me open the Shopping Week.

'Really now,' he replied, 'how interesting!'

And I don't know to this day whether or not he was serious.

Later 'Mattie' took me to see his charming old house, but on the way he stopped to buy a couple of rabbits, explaining that he dared not go home without them or he would be torn to pieces by his two black poodles! I began to wonder what sort of reception I, with no peace offering, would get. But all was quiet, and I had a most interesting time looking at Mr Matthew's wonderful collection of autographed photographs of stars of the past and present.

* * * *

In June I also made two attempts on the London to Brighton and back record. Though beating Marguerite Wilson's time at my first try, I wasn't satisfied. My second attempt was better, and I clocked 5 hours 2 minutes 11 seconds, in spite of an unlucky hold-up at Crawley level-crossing.

That Brighton road is a challenge to me. Should I ever embark upon another spell of record attempts I am sure it will be high up on my list.

1. A proud moment at the Cycle Show 1952

2. Speeding into Hyde Park at 3 a.m. (25 miles nearer to the London–Oxford and back record)

3. No stops for food between Edinburgh and London

4. Records at Herne Hill track

5. Lady Hailsham congratulates me.

6. "Cycling's" Diamond Jubilee Celebrations at the Royal Albert Hall

7. The bedtime story before I leave for a training spin

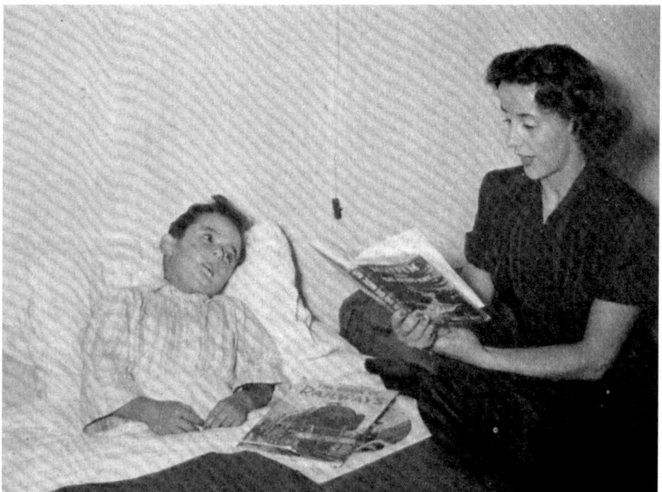

8. D. D. McLachlan, Publicity Director for Hercules, congratulates me in Edinburgh. Ken, my husband, is between us

9.

Showing Ronald Shiner how to ride a bicycle . . .

10.

but I would not care to demonstrate this one! One lesson from Steve Starr, and I mastered this 'old

11. Fun in Ireland: a heartening send-off from Cork to Dublin

12. Anxiety in Scotland: I lose my way in Glasgow

13. The night before the Big Day: I discuss the schedule for the 1,000 miles iwth manager Frank Southall – at 10 p.m.!

14. *Awaiting the word 'go' from timekeeper Alan Gordon at Land's End*

15. *Over 600 miles covered. Fatigue begins to tell*

16. *Refreshed after a short halt in the caravan*

17. Order from the Boss. I walk the 1 in 4 section of Berridale, 826 miles on – and company is welcome

18. John O'Groats, 11 p.m. Sweater, racing cape, brown paper – nothing seemed able to help keep me warm, as my resistance was lowered, on that grim third night of riding

19. John O'Groats just 12 hours and 130 miles later, and the 1,000 mile record in the bag too!

20. Land's End to John O'Groats and the 1,000 miles all behind us. Off to celebrate!

21. Activity behind the scenes, to enable one girl to break a record

22. Throwing 82 lb. around to get fit

23. Limbering up in our home gym

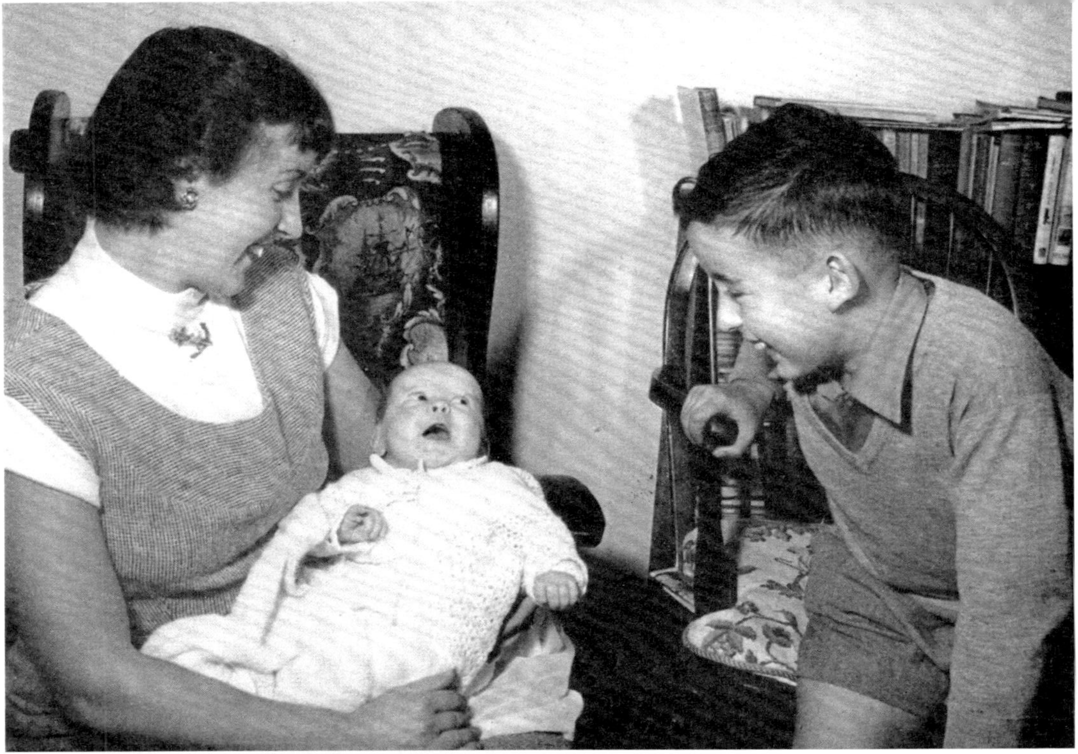

24. The girl who spoiled my 1955 career— Baby Louise at 7 weeks, with my son

25. But now it's 1956, and time to get fit again

CHAPTER TWELVE

A Spate of Records

Ireland now gave me a happy interlude. Record-breaking over there was a very different thing from what I had been used to. There were no advance publicity restrictions, and the public, who turned out to give me a send-off and cheer me along the route, could get a very good idea of the thrills which place-to-place cycling can provide. I hope that some day the same conditions will prevail in England.

We had travelled by plane to Dublin, taking my bikes along with us, and the intention was to start with the 168-mile Cork to Dublin record. Frank Southall asked Tom Walsh, the well known Irish record-breaker, for the wind direction.

'It's always south-west here' we were told, but when we emerged from our Dublin hotel it was blowing due west. That would mean a side wind all the way.

'Can't we go for another record to-morrow, and do the Cork to Dublin at a later date?' asked my manager.

'Sure, and whyever not,' came the reply. 'What about the Galway to Dublin?'

We studied the map and made for Galway, 134 miles from Dublin. That evening we enjoyed a beautiful drive along the glorious Galway coast.

Feeling very fit, I started off in the morning with

a motor cyclist riding 100 yards ahead to show me the route (this also is allowed under the Irish Cycle Corporation rules). On one occasion he actually took me off course, and he was very upset.

'Oi'll never forgive meself, Oi'll never forgive meself!' he kept saying.

'Don't worry,' I reassured him. 'I'd have taken that road in any case, even if you hadn't been there —so I'm no worse off!'

With the sun shining and a warm following breeze, I enjoyed every minute of that ride. After about fifty miles the young Irishman driving the van with my manager was greatly impressed by the speed I was maintaining.

'Gosh,' he kept repeating, 'how long can she keep this up?'

All along the route villagers were out in full force to see me through, with the local 'bobby' in control. Farmers from the fields shouted 'Good Luck' as I wended my way towards Dublin. Just outside the capital a police car was waiting to see me through the traffic, and when I reached the terminal point I was informed that I had averaged over 23½ mph for the distance—breaking the men's Irish record by fifteen minutes.

The police were extremely interested, and gave us full co-operation throughout.

'She's a darlin' goirl, a darlin' goirl,' said one officer, who seemed to express how they all felt.

The next evening we attended a track meeting, where the Irish cyclists showed their enthusiasm, and expressed their keen desire to see me into Dublin on my next record attempt.

After a day's rest we motored down to Cork. The morning papers there carried a big advertisement, stating that I would be starting outside the main post office at 8 o'clock the following morning. That produced a send-off from over 500 people who had gathered to wish me luck.

The police cleared a way through the excited throng, the timekeeper shouted dramatically (for the benefit of the crowd)—'Ten seconds to go, Eileen'. Then—'Five, four, three, two, one—Go!' To cheers and shouts, I was away. The wind was across me and quite strong, but there was no choice but to continue, as we were due back in England early the following morning.

The roads were very rough for the first fifty miles, and at one section, where repair work was in progress, the motor cyclist preceding me began floundering in thick sand which went on for nearly half a mile. He called a warning, and I had time to change into my lowest gear, which helped me to keep up a laborious progress through sand into which my wheels sank several inches.

News of my progress was given at intervals over Radio Eireann, which no doubt accounted for the enthusiastic cheering I received from villagers and townspeople throughout the journey.

Hundreds of people awaited my arrival at Dublin's main post office, and as the timekeeper checked his watch to credit me with another record some of the crowd grabbed me and lifted me on to the top of the car. Eventually, with police co-operation, we got back to the hotel where we celebrated our success.

* * * *

We flew back to London, and the great difference between the Irish and English ways was brought home to me like a slap in the face. For my first task now was to have another crack at the Land's End to London—a record that was really mine already, but which I had been robbed of in 1952 simply because of the W.R.R.A. rules on advance publicity.

'Let's get it over,' I thought, and set off the very day after our arrival at Penzance. Generally there was a gentle following breeze, but at times this dropped completely and rain fell intermittently. I was warm, however, and my breathing easy. My whirring wheels sped through Bodmin, Launceston, Okehampton, Exeter, over Salisbury Plain, and past Stonehenge to Amesbury, gaining on schedule all the way.

After twelve hours of non-stop riding I had covered a record distance of 238 miles, and my arrival at Hyde Park Corner, 287 miles from Land's End, in 14 hours 36 minutes 18 seconds, smashed my existing time by over two hours.

A small crowd of enthusiasts had gathered at Hyde Park—among them my father and Ken's mother—but I didn't stop. I had promised my manager that I would carry on for the 24-hour record. Waving happily to them all, I continued through the brightly-lit streets of London.

On the outskirts, with 300 miles covered, the first stop was made since leaving Land's End. It was getting cold, so my legs were given a gentle massage while I drank some hot chicken soup. Then I donned my warm training suit in readiness for the cold early hours of the morning.

The country seemed dark and so quiet after the bustle of London, with only an occasional car passing to relieve the monotony. Patches of icy mist appeared here and there, and how I welcomed the sight of the occasional small lamp which, waved in the distance, indicated that a helper was ahead with a lovely hot drink.

Few can imagine what a relief it is, in such circumstances, to see the first pale glimmer of dawn in the sky. It means the end of the struggle against sleep, and the constant straining to watch the dim road ahead.

The sun broke through and began to warm me again. At Norwich there was still about three-quarters of an hour left, so my wheels were directed towards Cromer. I was well on the way back from there to Norwich again when a blare of horns from the following cars told me my time was up.

In one ride I had seen the sea at Land's End in the extreme south-west and at Cromer on the east coast. The distances were checked, and it was announced that I had covered 442½ miles, beating the previous professional 24-hour record (held by Marguerite Wilson) by forty-six miles.

After fifteen days' rest I was ready to have another go at the London to York and 12-hour records. Remembering my experiences of the previous year on that route, I prayed for better conditions. The time of the start—8 a.m.—was more to my liking, despite the busier traffic in London, and I was able to ride hard right from the word 'go'. The journey was quite uneventful up to Doncaster—but between there and York are about half a dozen level crossings, and the chance of finding them all open is very small indeed.

I rounded a bend to find Frank, with Ken and a car full of helpers held up at one set of gates.

'Give her a chance' Frank shouted to the gatekeeper. 'She's on a record attempt.' But the man shook his head.

Frank fiddled with a small side gate, but although I was small enough to squeeze through it was doubtful if the bike could be got across. In any case there was a similar obstacle to be negotiated on the other side of the line.

Suddenly there was a roar, and we realized why the gatekeeper could not risk opening up. For the train that went by was the Flying Scotsman. The moment it had passed, the man lost no time in speeding me on my way.

A little further on I reached another set of gates just as they were closing, but at my pitiful 'Oh no!' the gatekeeper sportingly left a small gap for me to ride through.

A few more speedy miles and I was in York. Picking my way carefully through the narrow streets thronged with Saturday afternoon shoppers, I passed the timekeeper nearly an hour ahead of my previous record and carried on to attack the 12-hour figures.

After York the wind was right across the road, but I managed to reach Darlington with half an hour to spare, and when time was called at the end of my twelve hours my total mileage was 250½.

Except for the first level-crossing episode, I hadn't put a foot to the ground since leaving London.

* * * *

We ended our season with these records, and during the following winter and early spring all my efforts were directed towards one objective—to prepare myself for what cyclists know as the 'End to End'—that is to say, the formidable ride from Land's End to John o' Groats.

Invitations to cycling club dinners came pouring in from all parts of the country, and whenever possible I went to them by bicycle, often riding long distances.

I took on a bit too much, however, when I set out for the West Wales Cycling Association concert at Port Talbot, Glamorganshire, in bitterly cold conditions. Snow and ice covered the road in many areas, and I reached a point in the Cotswolds where cycling became impossible.

A lorry pulled up ahead of me. Would I like a lift?

Now, ever since I was a tiny tot, I had been warned never to accept lifts from 'strange men'. But this time I seemed to be between the devil and the deep white snow! The driver was a little man, and, remembering the many hours I had spent in weight-training, I took courage and gratefully joined him in the lorry. He turned out to be a perfect gentleman, even waiting at Abergavenny to make quite certain that I could get hotel accommodation there.

The road from Abergavenny to Port Talbot was quite rideable; and I cycled back next day with an escort of the Port Talbot Wheelers as far as Chepstow.

Whenever the weather was unsuitable for training on the road I indulged in strenuous spells with the weights and on my cycle rollers.

On many of these sessions in the gym I was joined

by two friends of mine—those eminent athletes Sylvia Cheeseman and John Disley, both British Olympic representatives. They, like me, believe that maximum efficiency in sport can be achieved only by keeping all the muscles of the body toned up.

For several years I haveenjoyed their companionship—yet I have never seen either of them running, they have never seen me ride.

On 9th April 1954 I set up figures for the newly-established London to Great Yarmouth record route. It turned out to be a hard ride, for thick white frost covered the countryside during the first half of the journey, and on occasions I disappeared from the followers' view into heavy mist.

The experience brought back to mind my first heartbreaking (though successful) attempt as a professional cyclist—the London to Portsmouth and back—when I had looked down from Hindhead to the white mist piled up on Frensham Ponds like masses of cotton wool. And when Frank Southall suggested that I try it again as a test of my fitness over a stiffer course, I felt somewhat dubious about my ability to tackle the Portsmouth Road so early in the season.

This time, however, great precautions were taken to ward off the cold—longer shorts, several sweaters, a layer of brown paper across my chest and back, and thick gloves.

Luckily there was very little mist about, and the run proved to be a much happier affair. Once more I was in a mood to appreciate—as only those who have cycled in the very early morning hours can appreciate—the wonderful peace and tranquillity that pervades the countryside as the sky begins to lighten.

I rode strongly to finish against a slight breeze, knocking a quarter of an hour off my own record.

Ken's mother brought my son Clive along to see me arrive, and we all enjoyed breakfast together.

'Funny, isn't it,' he said, with eyes wide open, 'Mummy popping down to Portsmouth and back before breakfast!'

You know I'd never thought of it like that . . .

Although I was the holder of both the London to Oxford and back records, it annoyed me that my amateur time was better than my professional. To put this right, schedules went in for another attempt on that stiff little ride of 109 miles.

Conditions were far from ideal, with a blustery wind dead against me to the turn at Oxford H.P.O. But, with a following wind to the finish, I passed the timekeeper back in London over ten minutes ahead of my previous professional record and more than a minute better than my amateur time which I had been so keen to beat.

Still getting me tuned up for my eventual End-to-End attempt, my manager took me to Scotland to try for the Edinburgh to London and the 24-hour records combined.

My previous 24-hour ride had been done on a cycle which had a frame constructed with very 'upright' angles, and the vibration from bad road surfaces was considerable, so that at the finish my whole body felt bruised. Frank Southall therefore decided that I should change to a bicycle with more sloping angles, and the difference in comfort was most marked.

Once again I was out of luck with the weather, for until Newcastle was reached a bitterly cold east wind hampered me and made the long climb over 1300-foot Carter Bar particularly tough. How unreliable our summer is! Although it was June the two sweaters I wore could not keep me from feeling chilly.

During the afternoon the effects of my hard struggle earlier in the day began to tell, and I kept finding myself dozing on my machine, whereupon Frank gave orders for sponges to be handed up as often as possible to refresh me. These had the desired result, and, with the wind now helpful, I began to regain lost time.

As night approached the wind dropped and rain began to fall, but I was riding strongly now and I reached the London G.P.O. 20 hours 11 minutes 30 seconds after leaving Edinburgh, with the record in the bag.

Though naturally tired, I was certainly not exhausted, and my manager was glad to see me ride past the timekeeper with the intention of carrying on for the 24 hours.

The route from the G.P.O. to the Brighton road (selected as the finishing course) was very intricate, but Frank called out 'Just concentrate on riding, kid. There'll be plenty of marshals to see you don't go off course!'

His organizing of that tricky section was truly wonderful. Never once did I have to hesitate at any junction or turning. Immediately I had passed, each marshal would be picked up in a car, hurried along a by-pass, and dropped at another awkward spot on my route.

Through the early hours of the morning I traversed the familiar Brighton road, and then I came upon Frank standing by the roadside.

'This is the spot,' he shouted. 'You've broken the record, with still almost a quarter of an hour left.'

Elated by this, I sped away, to the cheers and encouragement of the helpers who were stationed at half-mile intervals along the last few miles. My speed was over 20 m.p.h. when the car hooters called me to a halt, and it was calculated that my new record was 446 miles for the twenty-four hours.

On 12th June 1954 I tried for the Holyhead to London record, but conditions were hopeless. An unceasing headwind had slowed me almost to a crawl by the time I decided to 'call it a day' at Daventry.

The following week-end there was still a rough wind blowing straight across Anglesey, and on the chosen morning it was pouring with rain into the bargain. The timekeeper, Laurie Dixon, said the weather was impossible. But my manager insisted on a training ride to keep me limbered-up, and told the timekeeper he might as well start me officially—'just in case'.

Through the mountain passes of North Wales the wind struck me at different angles, and rain soaked me to the skin. When 100 miles had been covered I felt really 'under the weather' and stopped.

'I feel terrible' I told Frank. He was very understanding, and said that in the circumstances it would be better for me to come off. But—just like a woman!—I felt his sympathy to be a challenge and told him I would ride on a little further.

The rain stopped and it became warmer. My

watch had been taken from me so that I wouldn't worry if I were down on my schedule—and, with no inkling that at one point I was actually half an hour down, I plugged relentlessly on. At Stonebridge, Frank called out that if the last 100 miles could be completed in five hours, my time would be the fastest on record. Well, the wind had dropped; the sun was shining—it was worth a try.

The road is not easy from Coventry, but as I went on my determination grew. I began to put on pace, not letting-up for one moment. Those in the following car were amazed to see me climb Little Brickhill, which is quite a hill, at 21 m.p.h.

The Luton Wheelers marshalled me through Dunstable, and dodging through the traffic I was told that my deficit was now only five minutes.

I fought on and won. At St Albans I was two minutes up. Through Barnet and London I gained another eleven, to make a 13-minute beating of the previous best time.

So I broke another record—on a run which, at the start, I had never expected to complete at all. The helpers were delighted, and the timekeeper said he had never seen anything like it.

In all these testing rides—even during the 24-hour run—I had no recurrence of my old knee trouble, my body suffered no aches and pains, and I had proved to my own and my manager's satisfaction that I could 'take it'. I was all set for the longest and most arduous ride of my career—the End-to-End and the One Thousand Miles.

CHAPTER THIRTEEN

'End-to-End' Preparation

To pedal a bicycle from Land's End to John o' Groats would be a formidable undertaking for most people even if able to take their own time about the job. The prospect that faced me was a virtually non-stop ride of 872 tough miles in Britain's changeable weather.

Grim tales reached me of previous attempts on the End-to-End, as the route is known to cyclists. I heard of painful feet where continuous rubbing of the toe-clips had made it almost unbearable to cycle; of riders who could hardly bear to sit in the saddle, and others whose legs swelled to such a size that they actually rubbed on the pedal cranks; of those last fateful miles when the fatigued body is overcome with cold, and when many cyclists have suffered from lack of sufficient warm clothing.

But for over six months I had been steadily training, until I could sit on my bicycle for hours and pedal effortlessly with no discomfort whatsoever. One record after another had been attempted in order to build up my stamina for the longest of them all.

For some weeks I had been toughening my skin against saddle-soreness by dabbing it with surgical spirit regularly night and morning. The tops of my feet also received this treatment so that my shoes would not rub and find a tender spot. My shorts had large chamois leather seats, and before starting I spread plenty of Russian tallow on them, to stop any saddle friction.

During the winter months I had broken-in six pairs of racing shoes, which were now all perfectly comfortable (this in order to have plenty of changes if rain persisted). Quantities of spare wool vests, sweaters, and socks were also assembled—as well as some cool shirts, just in case we had sunshine in July!

Many well-wishers considered it advisable to get in as much sleep as possible beforehand, to prepare for the lack of rest during the attempt. However, Sir Adolphe Abrahams, the famous athletic adviser, explained that it was not possible to build up a sleep reservoir. This made me decide to live a perfectly normal life, and to go to bed at my usual time (between 11 and 11.30 p.m.) even on the night before the great day.

I had already proved my ability to cycle through one night. But what of the second? If I continued for the 1000-mile record, it would mean a third night also . . . but the thought of this did not deter me in the slightest. It was an ambition of mine to hold these records, and I looked forward to the test with great excitement. It was an adventure, and the idea of it thrilled me.

One day my manager, Frank Southall, and his wife called for me in the car. From London we cut across on to the End-to-End course and drove over the route right up to John o' Groats, to make sure of the quickest way through the different towns and villages. The scenery in the Highlands was, of course, magnificent—but the journey seemed endless even in a car. What would it feel like on a bicycle?

'Well, Eileen?' said my husband when I reached home again. I looked at him for a full minute, then—

'Ken,' I said quietly, 'It's a long, long way.'

Our headquarters were set up at the hotel in Penzance where we had stayed on previous occasions. There was a warm welcome from the manageress, and I was introduced to the chef who promised plenty of underdone steaks to prepare me for the job ahead.

Every morning for breakfast I had fresh fruit, a morsel of fish, and then a delicious steak. I would change then into my training suit, while Monty Southall (Frank's brother) and the helpers would strap my machine on to the back of his car for a drive to Land's End. Flat out, and usually with a following wind or slight side wind, I would ride hard to the Lizard, a matter of thirty-odd miles, to keep in trim. Frank and Monty, following in the car, noted how I was shaping. They found my hill-climbing excellent—and there are plenty of hills in Cornwall.

'Keep her happy' was Frank's motto during those final days of preparation. Although I trained seriously, at other times there was plenty of fun. Our party wore bright green and yellow woollen hats adorned with pom-poms. The lads in theirs reminded me of the 'kind-hearted rogues' of a favourite operetta—and I nicknamed them the Pirates of Penzance.

After lunch we would usually drive out to some pretty cove in the hope of relaxing in the sunshine.

But, such was July that year—even in the south-west—that every day we would lie fully clothed in a row on a beach from which we soon had to move because of the rain or the cold.

One promising afternoon a girl actually appeared on the sands in a swimsuit, and, encouraged, I felt for the 'bikini' that had stayed rolled up in my handbag for so long. Frank's sister, a staff nurse who was to attend me on the ride, held up her coat while I did a quick change. The sun felt wonderful, but Frank frowned and said 'No bathing'.

The sea looked very tempting, so I grinned at the boys and dared them to throw me in. They did—but I splashed about for only a few minutes. The water was cold, and it was so much nicer when you came out! Frank 'overlooked the incident', and I was quite content to look at the sea for the rest of the week and not be tempted in again.

We were waiting for the weather experts to give us a definite south-west wind forecast, but for the moment it appeared to be set in the west. On our third day in Penzance all the helpers caught a germ which made them feel 'under the weather'. When everyone felt better, I began to suffer from the same thing. However, this was soon put right, and Nurse Ruby Crew, Frank's sister, gave me very careful attention.

The next worry was an enormous stye on my eye. By a happy chance, staying at our hotel and sitting at the next table was an eye specialist who had shown great interest in our plans. He kindly treated my eye, and gave me injections against the recurrence of any similar trouble.

Many of the hotel guests were greatly intrigued to hear that a 'mere girl' was to ride a bicycle 872 miles. One gentleman approached Nurse Crew (a well-built girl, and much bigger than I) and said 'My dear, I just don't know how you can do it.'

'Do what?' asked Ruby.

'Ride a bicycle all those miles. Don't you ever feel tired?'

Ruby shook with laughter and indicated me:

'This is the little thing who does it!'

The guest thought we were pulling his leg, and was up early the next morning to see who really did ride the bicycle.

By now I was feeling on top of the world—eating excellently, and prepared to start at any time. Then at last Frank received a weather report which, though not perfect, seemed the best we were going to get for some time. I enjoyed myself right up to the last minute, went to bed at eleven o'clock, and slept well.

For breakfast I had the last of the steaks which had been cut every day for me by the local butcher's boy, who was a club cyclist and a keen fan of mine. Then I climbed into Frank's car for the short journey to Land's End, closely followed by Monty Southall and a carload of helpers and officials.

The timekeeper was Alan Gordon, who incidentally had timed the previous End-to-End attempt by a woman. Mrs. Mary Rawlinson, secretary of the Women's Road Records Association, came as official observer, and Ruby Crew was in charge of welfare arrangements. Maurice Tugwell and John Parsonson, both of Norwood Paragon Cycling Club, were helping Frank to feed and marshal me from start to finish. The other helpers had been detailed to travel down from London and to come in at Launceston, about eighty miles from Land's End.

A number of guests from the hotel drove to Land's End to see me off, and I received several 'good luck' telegrams from friends. Photographers buzzed around. Then Alan Gordon said 'One minute to go, Eileen.' The time had come for me to settle myself in the saddle for the longest and toughest ride of my life.

CHAPTER FOURTEEN

My Ambition Fulfilled

The morning was dull and gloomy, with the wind blowing not behind but across me, but I did not allow the magnitude of my task to worry me. And when, at 10 a.m. on Friday, 9th June, 1954, Alan Gordon said 'Off', I romped along the narrow twisting undulating lane from Land's End to Penzance as though I were on a training spin.

It wasn't long before I came upon the first of many well-wishers who, informed privately about the ride, were to cheer me on my way at numerous points along the route. In this case it was Dr Francis Jones, who had attended my eye at the hotel.

The wind was more southerly than south-westerly as forecast, and the climb over the long slopes of Bodmin Moor was at times very tough. My helpers were beginning to get worried, as the wind seemed to be veering south-east, right across me. The famous 'Jamaica Inn' was crowded with tourists when I went by, and, as one of the boys handed me up a drink, many cameras were brought into action.

An indication of my hard fight in the early stages was the fact that at Launceston I was over a quarter of an hour down on my schedule. It was here that my husband Ken and other helpers made their most welcome appearance. There were Stan Butler (Norwood Paragon Cycling Club), Jack Howe and

Ray Challis (Epsom C.C.) and Bill Cradock. From that point onwards one or more of them were by the roadside at regular intervals, with a drink, a sponge, and always a cheery smile and a word of encouragement.

The weather continued to deteriorate, and just before I reached Exeter (120 miles) cold fine rain began to fall. But, knowing that when completely soaked I would be able to stop for an entire change of clothing, I did not bother to put on a cape.

Exeter, where I was half an hour down on schedule, was as usual very busy indeed, but I managed to get through fairly easily. The road now took a more northerly direction, and so the wind was more helpful. I passed a happy group of cycling club folk on holiday from Manchester. They had stopped to give me a hearty cheer as I went by.

And now to join the helpers came Mrs Lillian Dredge of the W.R.R.A., the first woman ever to set up End-to-End figures. The large car in which Lillian was travelling was to be used by the helpers for 'by-passing' purposes, and was driven in alternate shifts by two chauffeurs who had been out on several previous record attempts.

Frank handed me up the first solid food of my ride. It was placed in a canister attached to my handlebar stem and consisted of sliced chicken breast and sliced banana. I ate them together, finding that the banana helped me to swallow the chicken more easily when my mouth was dry. Up to this point I had taken drinks of water and blackcurrant juice, to which glucose and sugar had been added.

By the time I reached Bristol, having covered 195 miles, the rain had stopped, but the sky remained very dull and overcast. The streets were thronged with crowds hurrying to evening theatre and cinema performances. But every crossroad, traffic signal, and pedestrian crossing on my route through the city was marshalled by more than 300 Bristol club cyclists, and I was able to carry on without a moment's hesitation. The huge task of contacting and briefing that army of willing helpers was undertaken by the late G. A. Widmann, a beloved figure in Bristol cycling circles who wrote about the game for many years under the pseudonym of 'Cotter Pin'.

Before Gloucester a very brief halt was made to put lights on my cycle, and a warm white sweater on me. I had been pedalling without rest for over twelve hours, and was about to ride into the first night.

It was moonless, but I had a slight following breeze and it was quite warm. With trusty helpers appearing at shorter intervals, it was possible with very little trouble to combat the desire for sleep.

After Worcester the roads became deserted, and as the trail of cat's eyes, illuminated by the headlamps of the official car following me, stretched out into the darkness ahead, a queer feeling of unreality came over me. The silence was broken only by the faint hum of the car and the swish of my tyres. The towns and villages had a deserted, haunted look, and when the road passed between avenues of overhanging trees I seemed to be riding through a vast tunnel.

At Whitchurch, just before dawn, rain started to fall steadily, but again I preferred not to put on a waterproof. Despite the gloomy aspect of the industrial areas of Warrington and Wigan in the early hours of a damp misty morning, I felt very high spirited. When this area was behind I should have done well over a third of my journey.

The rain ceased soon after Preston (382 miles) and a stop was made to enable me to change into dry clothes, for now I was beginning to feel the effects of the early morning dampness.

After passing Kendal I prepared to tackle the long climb to the summit of Shap Fell (1304 feet), but a broken gear cable forced me to change my cycle just before making the ascent. The change had its compensations, however, for the saddle of the fresh machine seemed even more comfortable than the original, and I decided to keep to it for the rest of the journey.

Though somewhat blustery, the wind was more or less favourable up Shap, and my speed during the five-mile climb never dropped below 10 mph, even over the final stiff incline for which I used my 72-inch bottom gear.

Not far from the top of Shap I had completed twenty-four hours' riding and had covered 432 miles. Just before Penrith a change back to my original cycle was made, but I kept to the second saddle.

It was here that I saw for the first time the caravan which was to follow me all the way to John o' Groats. Fully equipped with sleeping and cooking facilities, it was mounted on an enormous trailer drawn by a powerful lorry. The toilet was in a little hut standing on its own between the cab of the lorry and the van.

Gathered around now was a large group of helpers and pressmen expecting me to make a halt for my first rest since leaving Land's End. To their astonishment I sailed right past with a cheery nod of my head, for I was feeling fine and quite disinclined to stop at that point.

The outskirts of Carlisle (470 miles) were in sight before fatigue and cold forced me to indicate to the following car and the caravan that the time had come for me to rest my weary and chilled body at last.

The caravan pulled in, and I joyfully climbed up the steps into the arms of Ruby (Nurse Crew). She was an angel to me. But we had an understanding before we started that on no account was she to let me sleep when I should really be cycling. It was essential that she should be strict with me about this, and I promised whole-hearted co-operation.

While I sat by a gas fire warming my frozen limbs, Ruby served up some delicious hot broth. Then, after a change of clothing and a blanket bath, I had a short nap of fifteen minutes. Feeling wonderfully fresh and prepared to tackle more miles, I appeared at the top of the stairs, whereupon Monty Southall —in spite of my laughing protests—insisted on carrying me to my cycle to save every bit of energy.

Shortly after leaving Carlisle I experienced one of the worst patches of the whole ride. Torrential rain began to fall as the lower slopes of the 1000-foot Beattock Bank climb reared up, and to make matters worse the wind blew straight at me, flattening the grass and causing the rain to sting my face. A group of club cyclists approached from the opposite direction, flying along as if jet-propelled. Why could it not be like that for me!

I suffered greatly over that stretch. The strain was mental as well as physical, for here was I, pitting all my strength against the wind and the gradient, with cold rain chilling me to the marrow, and with the knowledge that there were still 350 miles to go.

Would I be strong enough to continue if such conditions persisted? The idea of giving in is quite foreign to my nature, but once or twice during that cruel climb I had to give myself a severe pep-talk, and John Parsonson told me afterwards that he had never seen me in such a state.

Conditions improved slightly as the mountainous area was left behind, although the wind kept on changing direction. I would be bowling along one minute, fighting into it the next, and then great gusts would catch my cycle on the side. It was late on the Saturday afternoon when Lanark (546 miles) came into sight, and for the first time since the start of my ride I was showing a gain on my schedule.

Another forty miles, and Stirling was reached. I well remember the glorious sunset that evening. The sky glowed rose pink, reflecting in all the windows and making the Wallace Memorial stand out in high relief against the background of its lovely wooded hill.

At Perth (612 miles) a brief halt was made to fit lamps and put on extra clothing again for the ride through the night—the second night. It was about here that I became conscious of a nagging pain in my right knee. Whether it was caused by the cold dampness, or by the strain of continuous hill climbing, I could not tell, but it persisted for the rest of the journey.

At midnight I passed through Bankfoot, having covered 625 miles, and pedalled on to Dunkeld and Pitlochry. It was near the latter that I suddenly came across a row of red lights strung across the road, and, as my cycling had by this time become almost automatic, I was at first unable to realize what it was all about.

Then I saw a lorry overturned by the roadside, and the policeman who was diverting the small amount of traffic told me that the accident had had fatal consequences. I asked his permission to continue on that road, explaining about my record attempt, and he sportingly let me pass. But in the darkness I had failed to notice that the ground was strewn with broken glass. My silk-sided tyres ploughed through it, and I prayed that they would not puncture. It was a great relief when I was clear of the debris.

My route now took in the famous Pass of Killicrankie, after which I entered the forests around Blair Atholl and soon began the long climb up the slopes of the Grampian Mountains. Through this second night the midnight sun lighted a strip of sky on the northern horizon, but all around me the mountains appeared like monstrous forbidding shadows, streaked here and there with patches of white—snowdrifts in the gullies.

The opalescent dawn began just before I reached the summit at 1500 feet, but with its arrival the temperature dropped still further until the intense cold was almost unbearable. Paradoxically, the harder I pedalled the colder I became, for the increase in speed made the frost-laden air lash my face, sting my eyes, and numb my hands and feet.

After a while my numbed feet gave me such pain that I was forced to stop. Frank appeared at once, and realizing the situation, whipped off his own thick socks and pulled them over my shoes. He then waited at the roadside, barefoot, until a spare pair of socks could be brought from the caravan.

Of course I was not the only person to be affected by the cold, and I felt very sorry for the helpers who appeared at intervals looking frozen, each hugging a flask to his chest in an effort to keep the drink it contained warm for me.

The bitter cold persisted as I began the downward swoop to Dalwhinnie. And now the continuous vibration of the handlebar had caused a huge blister to appear on the palm of each hand, compelling me to grip the bar with my thumbs only, in order to alleviate the pain. At last, feeling very miserable, I halted at Dalwhinnie. I had cycled 673 miles and had gone through two whole nights with but fifteen minutes sleep altogether.

I showed Frank my blistered hands, and without more ado he packed me off into the caravan for a brief rest while sponges were wrapped around my handlebar to absorb road shocks and vibration. During my twenty minutes in the caravan I warmed myself over the fire and then put on a plastic jacket to keep out the freezing wind on the rest of the gradual downhill route out of the Grampians.

Wearing two pairs of gloves, I eventually found a comfortable hold on my handlebar, and settled down again to the job of reeling off the miles. After dropping down through Kingussie and Aviemore, I had almost reached Carrbridge (701 miles) when Frank, seeing that fatigue, cold, and lack of sleep were beginning to tell on me, called me to stop.

Hot towels were held over my legs, and after changing my clothes I flopped out on my bunk. To feel the warm blankets cover my fatigued body was the nearest thing to heaven. I relaxed completely and fell into deep slumber.

After twenty-five minutes I was awakened and told it was time to press on. For once I would have given anything to be left in that warm bed, only too well aware of the cold unfriendly morning that awaited me outside. I weakened and asked for five minutes more. Ruby agreed, and on the instant I was asleep again. 'Time,' called the nurse. Opening one eye, I peered over the bunk, and, not realizing my five minutes were up, asked for another three. But Ruby, true to her promise, was firm.

The total duration of that stop was seventy minutes, only half of which had been spent in slumber, and it was 7.30 a.m. on the Sunday morning when I started pedalling again. Nurse Crew told me afterwards that she had never seen a long-distance cycling event before, and, though she had been duty bound to refuse me the extra minutes for which I had asked, she wept after I had left the caravan.

Ruby can rest assured that once on my cycle I felt perfectly happy and eager to continue. The helpers laughingly told me that they had taken full advantage of my stop—ten or twelve of them having tried to wash in a very small bowl of water. As the caravan had only a small supply, Frank allowed no more than the absolute minimum. Naturally a large amount of hot water was most necessary when I stopped, and Ruby had used some to wash my soaked clothes and dry them ready for use again. At times, when water supplies ran short, the chauffeurs were sent off with a few cans to fetch water from houses en route.

Soon after 9 a.m. on Sunday the 11th I came through Inverness, where several club people had turned out to speed me on my way. Nearing the town, I was pedalling away in the now brilliant sunshine when a motor-coach on a holiday tour passed me. Several of the passengers leaned out of the windows to give me a wonderful cheer, and I then remembered seeing them several hundred miles back. They had, in the meantime, stopped overnight at an hotel, and were quite amazed to see me still cycling.

With 730 miles covered, and still feeling very fit, I rode past Beauly Firth, then on to Dingwall, Evanton, and Alness, having skirted Cromarty Firth which appeared beautifully blue beneath the cloudless sky.

Now came the seemingly endless climb over Aultnamain. The boys had expected me to walk part of it, but I felt surprisingly strong as I slowly ascended to the 1000-foot summit. The helpers were dropped at very frequent intervals—not only to feed me but to help keep up my morale. The sunshine now being quite warm, I was glad of my short-sleeved sweater, but I still preferred to keep my legs covered by my training suit trousers.

From Aultnamain to Bonar Bridge and Dornoch the scenery was of infinite loveliness. I was gradually reeling off the miles, and though tired I felt quite confident of reaching John o' Groats.

Golspie and Brora came next, and the road now ran along the coast, with the sea stretching away on my right. I knew I was approaching the fearsome hills of the Ord of Caithness. Helmsdale was the first of the hills to be scaled in this area, and I walked up the short steep section which comes before the huge horseshoe-shaped curve climbing to the top of the cliffs overlooking the sea.

Shortly afterwards I swooped down to the valley at Berriedale and dismounted to walk up the other side. It had been decided many weeks earlier that I should do this. My bicycle could, of course, have been geared low enough for me to ride up the 1 in 4 gradient, but the energy I conserved by walking more than compensated for the slightly longer time taken. Moreover, as all the helpers walked up with me, I was greatly cheered by their company at a time when the 830 miles covered were beginning to tell on me.

Despite my fatigue, I was most anxious to know how Peter, the lorry driver, would manage his enormous vehicle with the caravan aboard round some of the terrific hairpin bends. I need not have worried, for he manoeuvred the outfit like the expert he is. But Ruby, in the caravan, had a really thin time. One minute she was washing up at the kitchen sink, the next she was thrown on to the bunk complete with practically everything BUT the kitchen sink. Staggering to the window she peered out to find the caravan perched over a 300-foot drop. This terrifying sight caused her to retreat hastily and concentrate on her job inside. No praise can be high enough for the wonderful work Nurse Crew did on that run.

From the top of Berriedale the road, lined with telegraph poles, rose and fell into the far distance. I can only describe it as like a carpet being unrolled and never coming to an end. Then, looking along the coastline, I perceived a headland jutting out to sea about twelve miles ahead. Under the impression that it was my goal, I let out a whoop of joy. Shouting 'I'm nearly there, I can see John o' Groats' I refused the drink which Maurice held up to me. But I took it when he explained that there was still a long way to go—though I didn't realise then that it was at least forty-five miles.

Near Dunbeath a huge curve up the hillside enabled me to look down on the road I had just covered and see the line of following vehicles with the huge trailer bringing up the rear. How nice it was to see them! I waved gaily, and the drivers waved back. Jack Howe told me later that my cheerfulness, when they knew I must be desperately tired, brought a lump to their throats.

As I plodded on, a cold grey mist began to creep over the sea, gradually blotting out the warmth of the sun, and the wind turned directly into my face. Still those telegraph poles rose and fell away into the distance each time I breasted one of the many hills. The miles were beginning to take their toll. It was impossible to keep warm. Putting on all my available jumpers, with Frank's enormous polo-neck sweater over the lot, I continued doggedly.

Passing Lybster (840 miles) I fought into a headwind, and now my pace had dropped considerably. The helpers said afterwards that I looked a forlorn and pathetic little figure struggling along. I was really ready for another sleep, but, doubting my ability to make up for lost time in the last few miles, I just kept going.

Ahead of me at Wick (853 miles) Frank and his helpers were smiling broadly, thinking it would be plain sailing from there. How wrong they all were! If only the wind over those final stretches had been a little kinder!

'How far is it?' I questioned the boys at every opportunity. Not having been to John o' Groats before, they couldn't give me a direct answer. I reached the top of a rise and scanned every inch of the countryside. But there was no sign of a building which looked anything like the John o' Groats Hotel. Just hills and still more hills. . . .

The sea appeared grey and unfriendly, and the whole aspect was one of gloom. The local people, however, having got to know that I was nearly at the end of my ride, came out to cheer me on. I saw a group standing on the brow of the next hill, and, though I would have given anything to have walked up the steep incline, I gritted my teeth and rode very slowly, to the hearty cheers of the assembled villagers.

Owing to the lie of the land, it was not possible to see the hotel until I was right by it, and no one will ever know just what the sight of it meant to me. The narrow road leading to it had been repaired in strips, and to traverse it caused intense pain in my overworked leg muscles. Being quite free from saddle-soreness, I relaxed my pressure on the pedals and rested my whole weight on the saddle until the road patch was over.

Then, on level ground, I sprinted to the time-keeper at the finishing point by the door of the famous hotel. I jumped from my cycle, and Ken, Frank, and all the helpers rushed up to congratulate me.

Alan Gordon had held the watch all the way from Land's End to John o' Groats for precisely 2 days 11 hours 7 minutes. I had broken the previous professional record by 11 hours 45 minutes, and my average speed, which included all stops and sleep periods, worked out at 14·75 mph

Everyone was jubilant, but the official observer, Mrs Mary Rawlinson, was very upset, saying it had been awful watching me over those last miles. She need not have worried. Though tired, I felt extremely happy. Many photographs were taken, and holiday crowds clustered enthusiastically round. Waving to them, I climbed into the caravan. Desperately in need of sleep, my one desire was to have a blanket-bath and completely relax in my bunk.

My manager came to talk to me. He thought it best for me to have a good sleep before continuing for the 1,000-mile record, which would mean going a further 130 miles. That may not sound very far, but it called for quite an effort after having cycled through two complete nights and right up to the third evening, with only one hour and a half of actual sleep.

Frank told me he was really proud of me. His instructions now were to relax until he called. When Ruby had finished washing me, I needed no second bidding, and dropped off immediately into a deep well-earned sleep.

After a time I awoke, and, hearing Frank's voice, called out to him asking if I should be prepared to start shortly. He was most concerned about my well-being, but agreed that, if I intended to continue, it would be better to start right away. I was keen to get going, so Frank rallied the helpers and sent them off to various points along the course.

Having rested 1 hour 48 minutes, I left the caravan again with plenty of clothing on to ride into the third night. At eleven o'clock (my usual bedtime) Monty Southall pushed me off. With shouts of 'good luck' ringing in my ears, I was away on what was to be the greatest trial of all: the fight against mental weariness.

CHAPTER FIFTEEN

Triumph and Tragedy

I was able only to roll gently away from the John o' Groats hotel. My muscles had stiffened, and it was a painful business getting them into motion at all.

The night was fairly dark, but out to sea the midnight sun lit a streak of sky on the horizon with a fiery glow, making buildings nearest the shore stand out darkly silhouetted against the brilliance.

Everything about that third night seemed unreal. I was riding over unfamiliar roads and had no idea of direction. The 130 miles I had to cover were in short 'legs': first to Castletown, then Reiss, back to Castletown, on to Thurso, Wick, back to Thurso, Castletown, and thence to John o' Groats. But so far as I was concerned it mattered not where I went. My job was to keep pedalling, and turn when directed.

But after some distance I felt it must soon be time to turn. Having seen no one, I peered into the darkness ahead—and, sure enough, there was a whole group of clubfolk by the wayside, with one man in the centre signalling me to turn. Thanking him, I put my foot to the ground in order to look back to see that the road was clear.

Immediately came a voice from the following vehicle: 'Why have you stopped?'

'I turn here,' I replied.

'No you don't, Eileen. Carry on.'

I was about to argue and point to all the people, when I realized there was no one there at all. I had, quite literally, been 'seeing things'. I was shaken; things must be worse than I had imagined. But in fact this sort of thing happened three or four times along those lonely roads, and quite often I waved to people who were not there.

Those final miles were a dream (or a nightmare). Hedges became rows of animals—polar bears—all manner of creatures. Beautifully coloured images would appear, fascinating to watch.

'I keep seeing things' I said, halting and speaking to the driver of the car.

'Don't worry, kid, we're all seeing things,' came the reply. 'Just keep riding'.

The driver was Jack Howe—and I learned that poor old Monty Southall was having a rest. He had been at the wheel all the way from Land's End. 'If Eileen can cycle, I can drive' he had insisted but, a quarter of an hour after we had left John o' Groats Hotel, he had collapsed over the wheel through sheer lack of sleep.

'If Eileen can cycle.' As I remounted, I wondered. Speed now was a secondary consideration; all my efforts were concentrated on keeping awake and forcing my legs to keep pedalling. But I didn't worry unduly; I knew that everyone else who had attempted the '1,000' had finished in the same state.

I continued to 'see things'. Larger things now. An enormous glass tumbler, lying on its side in the road, appeared from nowhere. I swerved to miss it. A car being driven at a terrific speed was heading straight for a wooden platform on wheels. Feeling sure there would be a crash, I shuddered, but the amazing contraption swung down and the car swooped over it. I can remember thinking to myself that Frank must have made it! It all sounds so silly now, but at the time it was only too realistic.

There was no doubt that I had reached a dangerous stage. A crash now, and the record would be thrown away, so, halting again, I climbed into the caravan. The mental strain was beginning to tell, and Frank told me to have a good hour's sleep and not to worry: I was hours up on the women's record.

About seventy of the 130 miles remained to be covered when I took to my bicycle again. I can remember riding very close to the grass verge for mile after mile. Officials in the following car, thinking I would crash, told me to try to ride more in the centre of the road. This was successful for a while, but my wheels were soon clipping the grass again. I seemed to be drawn to the verge as if by a huge magnet.

Occasionally, while pedalling automatically, I would doze off—to come-to again in a terrific swerve. My most troublesome patch seemed to be in the early hours of the morning, just as dawn was breaking. At one point I was crying through sheer exhaustion as I rode past Frank; but his worried look compelled me to call out that I was quite all right. He told me afterwards that he was not ashamed to admit that he himself wept when I had gone by.

The helpers did all they could to keep up my spirits. They appeared in comical hats, and each in turn proposed 'marriage' while running alongside.

The chauffeurs, Ted and Philip, ran for miles telling me funny stories and sometimes handing me bunches of flowers plucked from the grass verge. Anything—anything to break the deadly monotony....

Thirty miles, however, was all that could be managed before I stopped for another rest. Flopping on to the bunk, I told the nurse not to bother to change my clothing. Sleep was my only desire. Frank, worried about my ability to continue, came in to consult Ruby. The last girl to attempt the 1,000 miles had been unable to finish. Would I make it? It remained to be seen.

After an hour, Ruby roused me. Sitting up in my bunk, I whispered to her not to wake the helper, for I could see one of the lads asleep in the bunk opposite mine. Ruby insisted that no one was there, but I could see his face clearly and the outline of his body curled up under the blankets. Not until I had actually put my hands on the bunk did this trick of my imagination disappear.

Just before I started again, Ruby cooked me four rashers of bacon and two eggs. My hands being too sore to handle a knife and fork, Frank cut up the food and fed me, giving me a pep-talk at the same time. While he spoke, my eyelids dropped and my head fell forward over my breakfast. I was asleep again. Roused once more, I automatically chewed the food as Ruby popped it into my mouth, and although I was half asleep at the time I'm sure the meal did me the world of good.

The morning air was very fresh, the sky a glorious blue, while sun transformed the somewhat grim aspect of the countryside in that part of the world. I had got through my third night, and there were only forty miles to go. Not far now. I felt jubilant.

A herd of cows appeared in the road—real ones this time!—and, though normally I am rather cautious, on this occasion I shouted 'Giddy-up, there,' and rode on regardless. Luckily none of them kicked out; I have never been so close to cows before or since.

Lillian Dredge cheerfully waved me round the very last official turn. The final lap—about twenty miles to go.

The sea glistened in the sun, the grass appeared more green than ever before. A farmer shouted congratulations. I felt on top of the world again. My speed was increasing, and to Frank's amazement I averaged 18 to 20 mph over the finishing stretches.

A car containing some interested spectators got just in front of the official car, moving slowly and making it very difficult for Monty and the others to keep me under observation on those final critical miles. In the end Frank could stand it no longer. Leaning out of the window, he yelled at the driver—'For Heaven's sake get a move on!'

Not realizing what was going on behind, I took it that the remark was meant for me. Tired though I was, I fairly bristled with indignation. What a thing to say to anyone at the end of a 1,000-mile cycle ride! I shouted back over my shoulder 'What the devil d'you think I'm doing?' And, anger dragging from me that little bit extra, I did actually go faster for a short while!

Long before I reached it, my eyes were searching

for the little lane leading down to the John o' Groats Hotel. Regularly at intervals I would take a turning on my left, hoping it must be the one I sought, but a chorus of 'No!' from the men behind soon had me back on the main road again.

Not until I was practically there could the hotel's now familiar roof be seen. But at long last—at 11 a.m. on Monday, 12th July—I put my foot down at the door for the second time, to be greeted by Alan Gordon with the great news that I had completed the 1,000 miles in 3 days 1 hour, smashing the existing women's record by 10 hours 44 minutes.

Although the men's End-to-End record, held by Sid Ferris, was 4½ hours faster than mine, I had gained nearly two hours over that last 130 miles, and was thus only 2 hours 20 minutes slower than Ferris's '1,000'. In fact, mine is the second fastest time, by either sex, over this, the longest of all British road record routes.

* * * *

The photographers got busy again. Everyone was jubilant. Ken, my husband, was relieved beyond words to find that I felt perfectly all right at the end of the long effort. Joyfully I went into the caravan for a twenty-minute nap, but I felt too excited to sleep. Ruby gave me one of her super blanket-baths, after which I dressed in a summer frock.

It was quite a job zipping-up my dress and getting sandals on, for my whole body had become swollen by continuous effort over three days and nights. Having put make-up on and brushed and combed my hair, I went in to enjoy lunch with all my helpers who—for the first time since leaving Land's End—were well washed and shaven.

The manager of the hotel explained that it was customary for him to stand 'a pint' to anyone setting up a record of any description from Land's End to John o' Groats. Being a girl, I was given a choice, and I asked for a cherry brandy—which was promptly doubled to include the '1,000' record too!

After lunch I weighed myself on the machine outside the hotel, but returned to tell the helpers that it must be out of order. On setting out from Land's End I had weighed 7 st. 12 lb. and now (according to the machine) I was 8 st. 6 lb. The lads hopped on to the platform in turn, each reporting the loss of a few pounds, due no doubt to the lack of proper meals and the continual running about.

It seemed that there was nothing wrong with the machine, so I weighed myself again with witnesses. I could hardly believe it, but there was the evidence. I had put on 8 lb.!

Two hours after my 'finish', the imminent arrival was reported of the famous tandem tricyclists, Crimes and Arnold, who were attacking the End-to-End time for their type of machine. Our group were the first to congratulate them on smashing the record.

Most of us set off to London by road on the following day; but Ken, John Parsonson, and a few of the newspapermen returned at once by train from Inverness to get back to work.

After we had seen them off at the station, I called at a chemist's to find if anything were obtainable to soothe my legs.

'I've been for a rather long cycle ride,' I told the assistant, 'and my legs are swollen. Have you something to relieve them?'

The assistant looked most interested. 'I say, are you the young lady who has just cycled from Land's End to John o' Groats?'

I nodded.

'Your photograph has been in all the papers, and when I read about it I wondered how it would affect your legs. Do you mind if I look at them?'

I agreed, if it would help. He trotted round the counter and pressed my puffed-up calves gently, for he could see they were causing me discomfort.

'Hmmmm! I would have expected them to be very much worse than that,' he exclaimed.

He produced an excellent liniment which certainly did the trick, and under Ruby's instructions I rested as much as possible with my legs up. They were back to normal in three days, and—much to my delight—my weight gradually subsided as well.

On the way down to London, I asked Frank Southall to drop me at Coventry, for I felt sure my father and mother would be eagerly awaiting all the news of my ride. My joy turned to sorrow, however, when I learned that, while I was in Penzance awaiting the chance to start, my father had undergone a serious operation and was not showing any progress.

He had not been in the best of health for some time, but I was quite unaware that, just when my End-to-End attempt was imminent, his condition had worsened, necessitating the operation. On being taken to hospital, Dad had insisted that I should not be told, lest my natural anxiety should in any way affect my performance.

A second operation was again unsuccessful. Just three weeks after the triumphs which he had so eagerly hoped I would achieve, my father passed away.

I shall cherish the memory of his grand companionship during my childhood, his great enthusiasm and pride in my cycling achievements, and the love and help he gave me at all times.

CHAPTER SIXTEEN

Temporary Full-Stop

Two more records remained unconquered—the 25-mile and 50-mile. I 'finished them off', as Frank put it, in October, but the job was not so easy as all that.

The 50-mile course, which ran through Princes Street, Edinburgh, and finished along the coast near North Berwick, included nine miles of cobbles. And an unlucky skid and fall on a severe bend at Aberlady gave me a lot of cuts and bruises and lost me the record by one minute. And on the second attempt, a sudden storm made the journey a nightmare—for greasy wet cobbles and criss-cross tramlines had to be taken at top speed in the relentless rain. It was the only way to gain the record—which I eventually snatched by 1 minute 33 seconds.

The 25-mile run was happier, and, in spite of a strong cross-wind at times, I put all I had into this last record ride of all, passing the timekeeper in 1 hour 3 minutes 58 seconds.

So my story nears its end. To have been able to last out on long rides, right from the start of my cycling career, points to a natural stamina—but my speed was gained only by intensive and sustained training. I have been fortunate in my choice of machines and equipment during my decade of competitive cycling, and to my sponsors of the last three years goes my great appreciation for their encouragement, consideration and generosity.

Many of my rides would have been infinitely more hazardous and confusing had it not been for the help of literally hundreds of true enthusiasts of the game. At all hours and in any weather they turned out to marshal me through towns and cities and to give a shout of encouragement—so heartening to the lone long-distance cyclist. And to my End-to-End helpers I can never express my gratitude for the truly wonderful way in which they looked after me during those three gruelling days and nights.

Finally, there is Frank Southall. Formerly the greatest cyclist in Britain, he took on the job of managing my professional record attempts with a skill and efficiency that became a byword in the cycling world. In a very short time he had assessed my capabilities and acquainted himself with my idiosyncrasies—with the result that a state of one hundred per cent co-operation existed between us. Always solicitous for my well-being, and genuinely distressed when I was going through a bad spell, he had my whole-hearted confidence at all times.

With my final successes I had become the holder of all twenty-one professional cycling records on the books of the Women's Road Records Association, with distances from 25 to 1,000 miles. Little wonder that my helpers, who had come out in force on that final ride of the year—maybe of my whole career—organized a celebration in no mean fashion.

No sport, no movement, no organization of any kind can produce finer friends, or inspire greater understanding, loyalty, and unselfish enthusiasm than the great game of cycling. I thought of the thousands of unknown friends who had helped and encouraged me, and knew I hadn't let them down.

I thought, too, of the great crowd at the York Rally—the annual national rally of the Cyclists' Touring Club—which I had attended in August 1954, soon after my accomplishment of the 1,000-mile record. It was the Warwickshire branch of the C.T.C. which Ken and I had joined as newcomers to the game in 1944. Ten years later ten thousand enthusiasts of this, the world's greatest cycling club, cheered as I cycled round the arena with my son Clive—eight years old and mounted on his own junior bicycle—riding beside me.

It was a proud moment . . .

* * * *

And now, as I write the end of this story in the autumn of 1955, Clive has a new three-weeks' old sister, Louise. Once more cycling has given way to the claims of motherhood.

And I also have a very valuable addition to my collections of 'souvenirs' of my cycling performances—a magnificent framed illuminated address presented to me in October by the Women's Road Records Association on the occasion of the celebration of their 21st anniversary. I shall treasure it above all else, as it will always remind me of the organization which enabled me to achieve my highest ambitions.

Where is 'woman's place'? Is it, as my questioner at that Sports Forum in Coventry declaimed, in the home? Is it in industry, or in sport? If I have shown in my life that it can be—and successfully so—in all three, then I am happy.